ETHICS ON TRIAL

ETHICS
ON
TRIAL

Protecting Humans in Canada's
Broken Research System

JANICE E. PARENTE, PH.D.

DUNDURN
PRESS

Publisher: Meghan Macdonald | Acquiring editor: Russell Smith
Cover designer: Karen Alexiou
Cover image: solidcolours / istock.com

Library and Archives Canada Cataloguing in Publication

Title: Ethics on trial : protecting humans in Canada's broken research system / Janice E. Parente, Ph.D.
Names: Parente, Janice E., author.
Description: Includes bibliographical references and index.
Identifiers: Canadiana (print) 20250215829 | Canadiana (ebook) 20250215853 | ISBN 9781459755970 (softcover) | ISBN 9781459755987 (PDF) | ISBN 9781459755994 (EPUB)
Subjects: LCSH: Research—Law and legislation—Canada. | LCSH: Research—Moral and ethical aspects—Canada.
Classification: LCC KE3950 .P37 2025 | LCC KF4270 .P37 2025 kfmod | DDC 344.71/095—dc23

We acknowledge the support of the Canada Council for the Arts and the Ontario Arts Council for our publishing program. We also acknowledge the financial support of the Government of Ontario, through the Ontario Book Publishing Tax Credit and Ontario Creates, and the Government of Canada.

Dundurn Press
1382 Queen Street East
Toronto, Ontario, Canada M4L 1C9
dundurn.com, @dundurnpress

To my daughters, Adelaide and Halie Mei.

CONTENTS

FOREWORD

WHEN JANICE PARENTE INVITED ME TO WRITE THE FOREWORD TO *ETHICS ON TRIAL: Protecting Humans in Canada's Broken Research System*, I gladly accepted for three reasons. First, for several years I served in an advisory capacity with two non-profit organizations headed by the author: Human Research Accreditation Canada and the Human Research Standards Organization. I was particularly impressed by the dedication, expertise, and rigour exhibited in the setting of standards. Second, this book connects with my more than thirty years of work in human research ethics — as a policy-maker for the first edition of the *Tri-Council Policy Statement: Ethical Conduct for Research Involving Humans*, as a researcher examining governance in this area, and as a research ethics board chair and member — and then with my involvement in animal research protection. Third, and most importantly, as I have enunciated in numerous publications and reports, I share Janice's conclusion that Canada has a broken system for protecting human research participants.

In the first part of the book, Janice draws on her work as head of a contract research organization providing clinical research services and ethics oversight for for-profit pharmaceutical companies and subcontractors. This world is murky in two ways. First, it is an area largely hidden from public view, in which there are few public-reporting requirements. Second, there is a lack of effective oversight to deal with ethically questionable practices. The accounts presented in this book offer examples of significant harms to research participants. They also struck me as offering examples of ethically dubious business practices that I could have used in classes on business ethics. They raise questions about fair competitive business practices and unfair bargaining with temporary employees in the world of contract research organizations, such as backloaded incentive schemes for economically desperate potential research participants.

Starting this book with accounts of individuals in research resonates with the work my colleague Susan Cox and I did in our project entitled "Centring the Human Subject in Health Research," funded by the Canadian Institutes of Health Research. For example, we found a significant epistemic gap between what research ethics board members claim they know about participants in the research they review and what participants report they experience.[1] Issues concerning forum shopping resonated with me, as they connected the work I did designing the ethics curriculum for the Certified General Accountants Association of Canada, where independence and objectivity were central issues in management accounting and auditing.

This takes me to the second half of the book: Janice's analysis of Canada's current system of governance for research involving humans. The SFBC Anapharm cases concerning the death of a research participant and the outbreak of tuberculosis in separate clinical trials raise doubts about the Health Canada Inspectorate's diligence in human research protection. These cases were unusual in that the research practices of the parent company, SFBC, in both the United States and Canada actually came to light. The efforts of Janice's company to provide Health Canada with relevant information about significant protocol deviations were met with silence.

Citing Joel Lexchin's work, Janice identifies a root issue in Health Canada's conflicting roles as both a regulator and a promoter of Canadian health research. There are also jurisdictional issues, given the paramount provincial responsibilities for health. One bright spot in the 1990s and early 2000s was the role played by the Royal College of Physicians and Surgeons of Canada, under the leadership of Dr. Henry Dinsdale, when it joined the Medical Research Council and Health Canada to create the National Council on Ethics in Human Research (NCEHR). With leading experts in human research protection such as Pierre Deschamps, NCEHR established a rigorous national program for human research involving a regime parallel to the role the Canadian Council on Animal Care has played in animal research, including certification and site visits.

An underlying issue identified in the book is a kind of tick-box mentality when it comes to ethics in human research. Here, ethics is deemed as complete once research ethics board approval and informed consent have been secured. Ethics in human research is reduced to two paperwork items: a letter of approval from a research ethics board for the planned research and signed informed consent forms from the research participants. I have witnessed this mindset in the educational work I have done with researchers and governance experts. In 2000, at a gathering of authors who had prepared reports on various aspects of Canadian governance for the Law Commission of Canada, I was asked by a governance expert about my team's report. I said that it was about human research protection.

He said, "Oh, you mean research ethics boards."

I responded, "No, human research protection." This confusion of the instrument with its purpose is common in this area.

To combat this confusion, a paper my colleagues and I wrote describing the "life cycle of ethics" for research involving humans was incorporated into the standards developed by the Human Research Standards Organization.[2] This paper outlined a twelve-step cycle, beginning with priority-setting in research and with education in the science and ethics of research, and eventually culminating in quality assurance and improvement. Research ethics board oversight and research participant recruitment were presented as intermediate steps in a process designed to provide verifiable evidence of the practice of effective human research protection.

A key aim of Janice's book is the creation of a system of protection that warrants the trust of the public and research participants. In the work our team did for the Law Commission of Canada, we identified systems of oversight and virtuous learning loops as critical for creating such trust. Here, two points are crucial. First, all the major players benefit from such trust: research sponsors, researchers, research participants, and the end-users of research. Second, this can't be accomplished without providing independent rigorous oversight, which means giving up turf-protecting strategies. Janice provides abundant evidence of such territoriality. I personally witnessed turf protection during the meeting with research ethics colleagues across British Columbia that Janice describes in chapter 11. In that meeting, the director of research ethics at my own university, the University of British Columbia, deliberately ran out the clock in order to block other meeting participants from learning about standards and accreditation. This behaviour struck me as totally inconsistent with what should be expected from the representative of an institution devoted to the free and open discussion of ideas. Even more worrisome has been the persistent denigration by the Secretariat on Responsible Conduct of Research of the expert and important work done by the Human Research Standards Organization and Human Research Accreditation Canada. To that end, the Secretariat has consistently misled stakeholders and the public by labelling these organizations as "private," suggesting for-profit rather than not-for-profit entities.

The most disturbing revelation in this book is the recent limitation of the Secretariat's oversight of human research solely to federally funded research, explicitly ignoring externally funded research from foreign or domestic sources. A startling example of this type of research was the case of the "Texas Vampires," in which researchers from the Baylor College of Medicine in Houston went uninvited to Newfoundland and Labrador to gather, in a suspect manner, genetic samples from families of those with a particularly lethal form of cardiomyopathy. This eventually led to legislative action on the part of the province against such genetic-research piracy.[3] The Secretariat's sacrifice of oversight of externally funded research not only disadvantages research participants, but it also works against the collective interests of research sponsors, researchers, research institutions, and the general public.[4]

Instead of using the long-standing precedent of armslengthening animal research protection to an independent expert body — the Canadian Council on Animal Care — the Secretariat and the federal research funding agencies have ducked all action toward the oversight of human research and the protection of research participants. The question, then, in Canada is whether we continue with the status quo, resulting in more stories like that of Henri and the other individuals presented in this book, or finally act together to produce a more effective and independent alternative.

My hope is that this book will stir debate around Canadian human research protection and lead to meaningful action on the part of the research community and relevant authorities.

Michael McDonald, B.A., M.A., Ph.D.
Professor Emeritus of Applied Ethics
W. Maurice Young Centre for Applied Ethics
University of British Columbia

INTRODUCTION

YOU MAY RECALL A RESEARCH STUDY PUBLISHED IN THE *LANCET* IN 1998 THAT linked the measles, mumps, and rubella vaccine to autism spectrum disorder. This new knowledge created a seismic, worldwide reaction and incited prominent researchers in the field to scrutinize the study. Numerous flaws were uncovered, such as the study's small sample size (twelve children), the lack of a control group, and the speculative and unsupported nature of the study's conclusions. As a result, many epidemiological studies were undertaken, all of which debunked the original research.

This led to the paper's ultimate retraction by the *Lancet* in 2010.[1] By then, it was too late. The knowledge, albeit false, of the link between vaccinations and autism spectrum disorder had already harmed society. Skeptical parents stopped vaccinating their children, leading to outbreaks of the very diseases once controlled or eradicated by vaccines.[2] The long-lasting effect on society of this false knowledge was observed during the recent pandemic, when widespread hesitancy and reluctance to vaccinate hampered attempts to control and eliminate Covid-19.

———

Knowledge gained from sound research is fundamentally important for a functioning society. It can propel a society forward by improving and advancing many of its facets, like health, education, technology, innovation, economic growth and development, diversity and culture, and environmental sustainability. Given these profound consequences, the research from which knowledge is gleaned must be conducted rigorously. Researchers must abide by the ethical principles of research, including honesty, objectivity, integrity, transparency, accountability, and stewardship, to ensure that the knowledge that emerges from their work is valid and of the highest quality.[3] Research conducted on animals and humans must follow additional ethical principles, such as respect, concern for welfare, and justice.

Interventional health research, of which clinical research is an example, is a type of human research. It is not without risks. Researchers must ensure that it is conducted in a manner that protects research participants from harm and safeguards their rights and welfare. Failure to do so can have catastrophic effects, and considering what is at stake, society must employ measures to prevent misadventure.

Although Canada has developed policies and guidelines for the proper conduct of human research, there are enormous gaps in its oversight. These gaps directly enable acts of negligence and misconduct that adversely affect research participants.

———

I am passionate about research, especially human research. In high school, I excelled in math and science, and I leaned toward related disciplines in university, earning an undergraduate biochemistry degree and a Ph.D. in medicine (molecular pharmacology). I began my formal research career in drug development within the Canadian pharmaceutical industry before establishing my own human research company in 1992. My company, one of the first contract research companies in Canada, provides the pharmaceutical industry, the medical device industry, and the natural health products industry with clinical trial management services. This company enjoys a successful existence today under the name ethica CRO. In 1995, I expanded the company's services to include a private research ethics board, which currently operates under the name Veritas IRB.

In 2003, my research company was invited to bid on a study for a Quebec biotechnology start-up company called Biorthex. I presented to the company's board of directors the reasons why my company was best suited to run its flagship study. I laid out my arguments in order of what I determined to be most important — that is, that we adhered to the ethical principles of human research, had excellent operating procedures based on current regulations and guidelines, continuously trained our research team and routinely monitored our conduct, and did all of this efficiently to keep costs down. We won the contract based solely on costs. The victory was bittersweet.

The Biorthex study was invasive. It involved implanting a device between the vertebrae to promote fusion in individuals suffering from lumbar degenerative disc disease. To test its research hypothesis, the study required two hundred research participants. The first participant was enrolled in the study in December 2003, and soon after, participants began to undergo device implantation surgery at study sites in Quebec, British Columbia, California, and Tennessee.

In April 2004, we learned through a press release that Biorthex was restructuring its operations and was immediately suspending its research activities, including the study we were managing. As I sat at my desk reading the news, my thoughts turned to the research participants and what was going to happen to them. At the time of the press release, eight participants had already undergone implantation surgery. I tried to imagine their feelings of shock and uncertainty when they heard that the study had been terminated, since this was not a risk they had been made aware of before they consented to participate. Even though the study would soon end for them, the devices would remain in their spines for the rest of their lives.

By signing the informed consent form, each research participant had contractually agreed to be followed for two years by their study surgeon to ensure that the device was behaving properly and that they were not negatively impacted by the intervention. When I realized that Biorthex adamantly refused to fund this follow-up period, I immediately reached out to the research ethics board that had approved the study and to Health Canada for guidance on what tools existed to ensure that Biorthex abided by its commitment to the research participants. Both bodies were powerless against the will of Biorthex to terminate its involvement in the study.

My feelings of helplessness turned to hope when I remembered that all two hundred of Biorthex's devices were stored securely on our premises, except for a dozen or so that had already been shipped to the study sites. The devices were made of a porous titanium-nickel alloy and were worth a small fortune. It was no surprise that Biorthex desperately wanted them back, but I flatly refused to return them. In a manner of speaking, I held them hostage until Biorthex agreed to uphold its contractual obligations to each of the eight research participants. The details of the legal battle that ensued are not relevant to the story, but suffice it to say that Biorthex eventually got its devices back and all eight research participants were monitored as promised at Biorthex's expense.

Expropriating Biorthex's devices was not an opening shot across the bow. It was a desperate attempt to ensure that Biorthex would be held accountable for its actions and accept its serious obligations to protect the research participants' rights, safety, and welfare. That I resorted to a shakedown to force a clinical trial sponsor to fulfill its obligations points to the serious lapses in the good and ethical governance of human research in Canada.

In this book, you will read stories of fellow Canadians whose lives were tragically impacted through their participation in research. You will journey through the evolution of the ethical principles of human research and see how these principles were loosely manifested into an ineffective governance system for human research in Canada, a system that does not hold accountable those responsible for inflicting heart-wrenching harms.

1

A SUSPICIOUS DEATH

THE MORNING OF SEPTEMBER 20, 2005, DAWNED LIKE ANY OTHER. MY YOUNG children needed to be loved, entertained, fed, washed, dressed, and safely delivered to their respective schools and daycares, on time, lunches in hand. I was particularly anxious, and maybe even distracted, that morning as the hour of what I anticipated to be a very stressful meeting approached. My colleagues and I were meeting with SFBC Anapharm at its office in Montreal. SFBC Anapharm was a contract research company and long-standing client of our research ethics board. The purpose of our meeting was to provide SFBC Anapharm with an ultimatum: make efforts to reform its current research practices or we would pull our services.

The drive to the SFBC Anapharm test facility from my last offspring drop-off took only ten minutes. I parked at the back of the Wendy's restaurant next door on Decarie Boulevard and entered through the test facility's main doors.

I like to imagine that I encountered a lovely man as I entered the test facility, a man with a gentle demeanour and kind smile. I picture him holding the door open for me and the two of us engaging in casual conversation. He introduces himself as Henri, and I happily stop to speak with him. I notice that Henri seems unwell and is having difficulty maintaining his balance. As he clutches the handrail to stay upright, I ask him if he is feeling okay. He replies that he is having some trouble, and I guide him to a comfortable chair and summon help. Together we wait for emergency care to arrive.

Regrettably, I never met Henri. Our paths did not cross that morning, even though we were at the SFBC Anapharm test facility at the exact same time, one of us entering and one of us leaving.

HENRI AT HIS END

In another part of the city, a woman named Jeanne waited in her living room. The house was quiet except for the *tick, tick, tick* of the pendulum swinging in the floor clock. Jeanne sat motionless, monitoring the passing time by the clock's chimes and strikes. It was almost 10:00 a.m. She nervously held her coffee cup with both hands to resist the urge to smoke another cigarette. She was overwhelmed with concern for her loving Henri. He hadn't been feeling well and had complained to Jeanne that he felt like he had the flu. That morning, he'd said he felt dizzy and that he was sweating and experiencing hot flashes.

Jeanne heard the key in the lock of the front door. Henri was home. Elated, she ran to greet him as the door opened. Henri, pale, stood in the door frame. It took every ounce of energy for him to remove the key from the lock. As he reached out to embrace Jeanne, Henri lost his footing and lunged toward her, causing them both to fall to the floor. Jeanne managed to wriggle out from under Henri to call 911.

Jeanne placed a cold cloth on Henri's head. He was barely conscious. She spoke to him in her gentle way about family and upcoming plans, like their trip to Florida in the winter. Paramedics arrived at 10:28 a.m. and immediately began life-saving measures, which they continued all the way to the hospital. Henri's death was marked at 11:20 a.m. at LaSalle General Hospital. The cause of death was recorded as a probable myocardial infarction, or heart attack.

Henri had walked into the SFBC Anapharm test facility that morning because he was participating in a clinical trial. Research participants like Henri are, to some, invisible, contributing to the clinical trial as sources of data points. But to those who know and love them, they are anything but mere statistics.

HENRI AT HIS BEGINNING

Henri was born on the first day of spring in 1930 in the community of St. Lupicin, Manitoba. He was the seventh of twelve children born to Ernest and Marie. Henri's Manitoba lineage dates back to the province's founding. In fact, Louis Riel was the godfather of Henri's grandmother Marie Alexandrine.

Approximately two hundred families, mostly first-generation Europeans, lived in the area surrounding St. Lupicin at that time. There was one Roman Catholic school in the town, where nuns taught the children, boys on one side of the schoolroom, girls on the other. Children started school when they were six years old, and since most families farmed, they usually began working weekends on the farm as early as twelve years old. During the Great Depression, Henri's family was poor, like most families in the area. Ernest could produce approximately fifty bushels per acre of barley in those days, which was quite respectable. But with a family of fourteen to feed, their food supplies were close to depleted by the time spring rolled around, so meals were rationed.

The family home was typical for its day, an uninsulated log structure with a sloping roof. On the first floor, the living and dining rooms were centred around an open fireplace. The living room doubled as a bedroom for Henri's parents. The children slept two or three to a bed on the second floor, with a curtain separating the girls' and boys' beds. Attached to the house was Henri's grandparents' original house, which now served as a kitchen.

Life was very hard for Henri in St. Lupicin. For whatever reason a parent might despise their own child, Ernest despised Henri. From the time Henri was a young boy, Ernest capriciously deprived Henri of his education whenever he needed help on the farm. He worked Henri to the bone, giving him the most physically demanding and demeaning tasks. One of Henri's jobs was to feed the pigs and clean their pen, which contained fifteen to twenty pigs at any given time. On one occasion, a pig escaped while Henri was cleaning the pen. Its speed and stamina led to a three-hour chase before Henri was able to return it to the pen. His accomplishment was not rewarded, though. After beating Henri, Ernest made him work in the dark to make up for the lost hours of chores.

To avoid getting caught by one of their father's wicked blows, the other children stopped playing with Henri. Even his mother, Marie, displayed her love only during clandestine encounters with him. Winter mornings were especially comforting for Henri. He, his mother, and his sister Thérèse would rise before the rest of the house's inhabitants to feed the wood stove and prepare hot chocolate, fresh bread, and porridge for the family. By the time Ernest was awake, Henri had already received the emotional and physical nourishment he needed to sustain himself for whatever the day had in store for him.

Henri retreated from the family, finding solace in books. He loved literature, poetry, and science. He had an amazing ability to memorize text, and his teachers often called upon him instead of reaching for a dictionary, an encyclopedia, or the Bible. He could speak English and French fluently. Henri was not a skilled farmer like his brothers. He was an artist, and this angered Ernest even more.

ESCAPE FROM ERNEST

Henri grew to become a handsome man. He had jet-black hair and dark eyes, and he was lean and fit. His smile was shy and inviting. He towered over most of the men in the family, including Ernest.

Henri left his home in St. Lupicin in 1951, on his twenty-first birthday, never to return, having reached the age of majority. He had a few dollars in his pocket and the hand-me-down clothes on his back. He had patiently and quietly waited for this day from the time Ernest had first beat him. Before walking away from his family, he stood atop an inverted steel pail in the living room and gave a speech. He recounted a few meaningful happy memories and made sure everyone in the room knew that he loved them. On this day, Henri harboured no resentment for them. Marie and Henri's siblings would never forget that heart-wrenching speech and how they pleaded with him to reconsider his decision.

As Henri walked down the laneway to the country road, Ernest called out to him. Henri stopped and waited for his father to catch up to him. With a smile meant only for Henri, Ernest stood silently staring at him. Then he offered Henri a bit of money. As they shook hands, Ernest smiled again and then turned and walked back to the house. Nine days later Ernest died.

Henri walked to town and then continued walking east to Highway 3. From there he hitchhiked to Winnipeg, where he bought some lunch. He made his way to the Trans-Canada Highway and hitchhiked eastward through Kenora and Vermilion Bay, spending the night in a motel in Dryden. The next morning he continued his journey, passing through Thunder Bay and stopping in Wawa for the night. He arrived in Sudbury early the next evening and, with very little money remaining, found a place to sleep that cost him nothing: an unlocked car.

During the day, Henri looked for work. And at night, Henri looked for a car to sleep in. This routine came to an abrupt end one night when a man found Henri sleeping in his car and called the local RCMP. The police did not arrest Henri. Instead, they brought him to the Sudbury police station and gave him a warm bed for the night, and for the next night and a few nights thereafter.

Henri's older brother Leo, desperate to tell him about Ernest's demise, travelled to St. Lupicin to look for him. No one had seen Henri for days. Leo visited the local police station to see if they could help him with his search. A few days later, a telegram was delivered to Leo at the family home. It was from the RCMP. They had located Henri at the Sudbury police station, where he was a temporary lodger. Based on the telegram, Leo realized that Henri was never coming home, even for Ernest's funeral.

GLORY DAYS

Unable to find work in Sudbury, Henri made his way back to Winnipeg. He landed a job at the Manitoba Pulp and Paper Company in Pine Falls, where he worked as a labourer for two years. While he was there, he met a beautiful woman named Susan and began dating her. They soon fell in love, and in 1953, when Henri was twenty-three years old, they were married. Henri and Susan journeyed east to Thunder Bay, where Henri joined the Royal Canadian Air Force. He trained as a radar technician, an occupation in great demand across the country at that time.

In the 1950s the threat of a Soviet bomber attack on North America precipitated a partnership between the Royal Canadian Air Force and United States Air Force to build the Pinetree Line, a network of early-warning radar stations that extended from Newfoundland to Vancouver Island along the 50th parallel. Concerns about whether the Pinetree Line could provide enough warning time to launch a counteroffensive attack led to the construction of the Mid-Canada Line along the 55th parallel. The

Mid-Canada Line was an effective warning beacon, but it failed to provide information on the potential targets of an attack.

The Distant Early Warning Line was proposed to overcome the limitations of the previous two lines. It soon became the most capable of the three radar lines. Constructed in the Arctic, it was far enough north to provide hours of advance warning, and because of the type of radar system it employed, it could both detect and characterize an attack effectively, making the other lines obsolete.

Up until 1957 Henri worked on both the Pinetree and Mid-Canada Lines, and his job took him and Susan to various regions across Canada. With the introduction of the Distant Early Warning Line, Henri was expected to relocate to the Arctic. Although this work would have been extremely fulfilling, he and Susan already had one child and Susan was pregnant with their second. Henri knew he had to put his family above his career, so he made the difficult decision to request another post, even if it meant that his duties would change. The air force relocated Henri to a Canadian Forces base in Saint-Hubert, on the south shore of Montreal. There Henri was responsible for the general maintenance of the airplane hangars.

Henri and Susan made their home in Saint-Hubert, and by 1965 they had four children: two boys and two girls. Most of Henri's siblings also ended up in the Montreal area, and they welcomed Henri, Susan, and the children into their families. Henri even began to make routine phone calls to his mother at her home in Notre-Dame-de-Lourdes, Manitoba.

Henri's job was neither challenging nor intellectually stimulating, and he did not take pride in it. His despondency led to him being late for work or missing work altogether. He became a regular at the Blue Bonnets Raceway in Montreal, betting on horses. He studied the statistics on what makes a winning horse, sure he would find the critical factor for success.

Susan did not have a job outside the home, and Henri's paycheque barely covered the family's expenses. Henri spent what little savings the family had betting on the horse races. They were unable to make ends meet, and Susan could not get Henri to stop gambling, so when their youngest son was eight years old, she started working outside the home in order to bring in extra money.

In 1975 the air force released Henri due to his irregular and sporadic work attendance. They offered him a severance package, which Henri immediately deposited into a bank account for Susan. His gambling addiction eventually destroyed his marriage, and he soon found himself divorced and sleeping on a couch in Leo's Montreal basement.

HENRI'S BELOVED JEANNE

Henri and Jeanne's love story began in the late 1970s. They were both in their forties, divorced, with four children each between the ages of nine and eighteen years. During their time together, Henri was devoted to Jeanne and supported the family as best he could. However, even on the best of days, the lure of the racetrack was an invincible force in Henri's life.

For the most part, Henri and Jeanne lived very modestly. By the time their last child was out of the house, they'd managed to scrape together enough money to spend a bit of time in Florida during the cold Montreal winters.

Henri was in relatively good health. He had a heart condition that landed him in hospital in the 1990s, but it was stabilized by medications that he took at breakfast, lunch, and dinner. His sister Thérèse recalls Henri taking his pills before dinner during her many visits with Henri and Jeanne at their home near the time of his death.

When Jeanne was eligible to receive Old Age Security, she purchased a small, ten-thousand-dollar insurance policy on Henri's life. She was worried that she would not be able to pay off Henri's debts and give him a decent funeral without it.

SFBC ANAPHARM

Henri was seventy-five years old when he decided to participate in a clinical trial in order to be able to offer financial help to one of his children. He convinced Jeanne that it was a quick and easy way to make a bit of money. Although he didn't recall the specifics of the study, Henri told Jeanne that he would be paid $1,160 for a two-night stay at the SFBC Anapharm test facility, located a short drive from their Montreal home.

In those days, SFBC Anapharm was a contract research company that specialized in the management of early-phase clinical trials out of its test facilities in Montreal and Quebec City. "Early-phase" refers to clinical trials conducted in the first two phases of drug development. Phase 1 drug trials are conducted to determine the maximum tolerated dose of the drug under investigation — that is, the highest dose that can be administered without causing unacceptable side effects. This is how researchers establish the appropriate dosage levels for subsequent studies. The goal of Phase 2 research is to determine how safe the drug is and how well it is tolerated and to get a preliminary picture of its therapeutic efficacy. Phase 2 trials are usually conducted in patients with the specific disease or disorder the drug is targeted to treat.

Every drug on the Canadian market, except generic drugs, has undergone early-phase testing. Generic drugs are replicas of brand-name drugs. They have the same active ingredients as the brand-name drugs, but may differ in how they are formulated and manufactured. In Canada, approximately three-quarters of all prescriptions filled are for generic drugs,[1] and because generic drugs don't have to undergo the costly multi-year, multi-phase clinical trials that brand-name drugs do, manufacturers can sell them at far cheaper prices. This doesn't mean that generic drugs don't undergo any testing at all, though.

For a generic drug to be approved by Health Canada for sale, it must undergo clinical trials to prove that it is bioequivalent to its brand-name counterpart. Two drugs are said to be bioequivalent if there are no clinically significant differences in their bioavailability. That is, the two drugs must release the same amount of active component into the bloodstream at the same rate and with the same quality.

Bioavailability is a measurement of the rate and extent to which the active component of a drug is absorbed into the bloodstream and becomes available at the site of action. Once the drug has entered the body, a series of accurately timed blood samples are collected in order to create a graph of the amount of the active component in the blood versus time. These data are used to reflect how quickly the active component is released and how quickly it is absorbed from the gastrointestinal tract, as well as how quickly it is metabolized, distributed, and eliminated. Two main pharmacokinetic variables are measured from these data. Based on international consensus, for most drugs, the generic and brand-name drugs are considered bioequivalent if there is no more than a 20 percent difference between their ratios of these pharmacokinetic variables.[2] It is important to recognize that this test of bioequivalence only concludes that the drugs are not different from one another, not that they are the same. In other words, bioequivalence studies provide indirect evidence of the safety and efficacy of a generic drug.[3]

Henri was slated to be enrolled into a clinical trial that would examine the bioequivalence between two types of fifty-milligram tablets of bicalutamide, a drug used to treat prostate cancer. One, the reference formulation, was a brand-name formulation called Casodex. The other, the test formulation, was a generic formulation made by Genpharm Inc. For the trial, SFBC Anapharm needed to enrol forty-eight "healthy volunteers," all men eighteen years of age or over.

Before the clinical trial commenced, Henri was screened to see if he qualified. This session took place on September 3, 2005, at 10:00 a.m. After signing an informed consent form for the screening, Henri was asked questions about his general health, his medical history, and any medications he was taking. His vital signs, including blood pressure, pulse rate, respiratory rate, and oral temperature, were taken. An electrocardiogram and various blood and urine tests were also performed, and SFBC Anapharm determined that the results were normal or not clinically significant.

In my opinion, however, one test result was noteworthy: the presence of inspiratory rales. Inspiratory rales are crackling sounds that can be heard through a stethoscope. They correspond to the opening of collapsed airways in the lungs due to the presence of fluid. There are many reasons why fluid could be present in the airways, including heart disease and pneumonia. In Henri's case, inspiratory rales were present on September 3, but they were deemed to be not clinically significant at 5:03 p.m. on September 9, the exact time and day that Henri was enrolled in the clinical trial. Henri did not disclose to SFBC Anapharm that he had a heart condition that was stabilized by medications.

In the late afternoon of September 9, Henri arrived, overnight bag in hand, at SFBC Anapharm's test facility on Decarie Boulevard. After signing an informed consent form for the study, Henri was taken to his allocated sleeping area and was cautioned that he could not eat anything until the following day. In the morning, Henri ate his assigned breakfast, and a blood sample was taken. At 9:12 a.m., Henri was administered a fifty-milligram oral dose of bicalutamide. Although he did not know which formulation he was receiving, Henri was randomly assigned to the reference group and given Casodex.

Sixteen blood samples were taken from Henri over the next thirty-six hours, and then he was allowed to go home. Unless Henri had smuggled his heart pills into the facility, he would have missed seven doses of the medication he needed: three doses each day for just over two days. Henri returned to the facility to have blood samples taken on September 12, 13, 14, 15, 17, and 20, but he was not required to stay overnight. At each of these visits, Henri was asked a number of questions about his general health condition. He was asked if he had eaten or drunk anything that contained specific prohibited products; if he had experienced any new health problems or taken any medications he hadn't reported at the start of the study; if he had donated blood or plasma during the study; and if he had smoked more than twenty-five cigarettes per day. It was recorded that Henri answered no to all of the questions at each visit.

Even though SFBC Anapharm had a medical doctor on site, Henri was not given a physical examination nor were his vital signs assessed at any of these study visits. The report from his last visit, on September 20, the day of his death, states that Henri provided a blood sample at 9:12 a.m. It would have taken him between twenty-five and thirty minutes to get home from the SFBC Anapharm facility after the visit. Henri collapsed as soon as he walked through his front door, at around 10:00 a.m., and he was pronounced dead at 11:20 a.m. It is very difficult to believe that Henri showed no signs or symptoms of distress at the SFBC Anapharm test facility that day.

Jeanne told her family that Henri had not been feeling well since September 11, just one day after he'd received the dose of bicalutamide. She described Henri as having the flu, yet he also complained of frequent hot flashes, dizziness, and sweating. He joked to Jeanne that maybe he was going through menopause.

BICALUTAMIDE

Bicalutamide is a non-steroidal anti-androgen used to treat prostate cancer. It binds to androgen receptors without activating gene expression. It is called a receptor antagonist because it prevents other androgens from binding to the androgen receptors to initiate the gene expression cascade. Its mechanism of action causes apoptosis, or death, of androgen-dependent cells. This is the drug's aim when targeting cancer cells, especially prostate cancer cells.

The informed consent form for the study listed flu-like symptoms, hot flashes, sweating, and dizziness among the many common side effects of bicalutamide. Heart problems, including heart attack, were also listed.

HENRI'S AFTERLIFE

Henri's next study visit was scheduled to take place on September 24. In her grief, Jeanne telephoned SFBC Anapharm on the morning of September 26 to report Henri's death. She was passed from one person to another until, finally, a man's voice came over the phone. The man, who didn't introduce himself to Jeanne, expressed his condolences and immediately disclaimed that SFBC Anapharm and Henri's participation in the clinical trial bore any blame for Henri's death. The man warned Jeanne not to disclose that Henri had been participating in a clinical trial at the time of his death, and he told her that she should not have an autopsy done. He cautioned her that autopsy results could jeopardize a life insurance payout. Jeanne shared this conversation with some of Henri's brothers and sisters.

There was a viewing for Henri at the Salon Funéraire Alfred Dallaire in LaSalle before his funeral service at the Saint Catherine Labouré Church. Then Jeanne had Henri's body cremated. As she had hoped, the proceeds of the life insurance policy she had purchased covered Henri's funeral expenses and his outstanding debts.

ETHICAL OVERSIGHT

The SFBC Anapharm study that Henri participated in was conducted under the auspices of our company's research ethics board. At 11:00 a.m. on October 3, 2005, we received an email from SFBC Anapharm containing a two-page initial serious adverse event report that summarily described Henri's death as not related to the study drug. Despite the notice on the adverse event report form stating that all serious adverse events must be reported to the research ethics board within twenty-four hours of notification, SFBC Anapharm provided no explanation for the eight-day delay in reporting. Henri's death was the outcome of a probable myocardial infarction, and this constituted a serious adverse event that fell under the twenty-four-hour reporting requirement.

At the time, Dr. Barry Brown was the chair of our research ethics board. On October 4, having reviewed the serious adverse event report, he emailed a letter to SFBC Anapharm requesting a copy of Henri's autopsy report and follow-up information about the study drug's relatedness to the serious adverse event.

After we made many attempts to obtain a response to the letter, SFBC Anapharm finally provided a follow-up report two months later, on December 7. The report contained vague information on Henri's death and the events that led up to it, which raised even more concerns from Dr. Brown and other members of the research ethics board. On December 19, the board requested the following information from SFBC Anapharm and the study's sponsor, Genpharm Inc.:

- justification as to why SFBC Anapharm deemed that Henri's death was unrelated to the study drug, given that heart attack was listed as a risk in the product information and on the informed consent form;

- a true copy of all case report forms for Henri (for the complete screening and baseline and all follow-up visits), especially the physical exam information collected on the day of his death;
- true copies of records from LaSalle General Hospital;
- a true copy of Henri's death certificate; and
- rationale for why an autopsy was not performed.

The board requested a response by December 23. At the end of the day on December 23, we received an email letter from SFBC Anapharm's medical director. It contained four sentences. In the last sentence, the medical director attempted to convince Dr. Brown that silent coronary disease is common in people in Henri's age group, and since Henri's death occurred ten days after taking fifty milligrams of bicalutamide, the medical director was sticking with his judgment that it was unrelated to the study drug.

The half-life of bicalutamide — that is, the time it takes for its concentration in the body to be reduced by half — is between seven and ten days. Based on its half-life, Henri could have had up to twenty-five milligrams of bicalutamide in his body around the time of his death. SFBC Anapharm had these important data because Henri had submitted a blood sample to the company two hours before he died. To assist in its determination of causality, all SFBC Anapharm had to do was look at the data to determine exactly how much bicalutamide Henri had in his blood on the day he died.

SFBC Anapharm's medical director pointed to Henri's age as the responsible factor in his death, yet he took no responsibility for enroling a seventy-five-year-old research participant into a clinical trial without safeguarding his rights, safety, and welfare.

SEARCHING FOR ANSWERS

Henri's family was suspicious about the circumstances surrounding his death. They suspected that the clinical trial played some role in his demise. SFBC Anapharm was not forthcoming with answers to their questions, and any clues about the cause of Henri's death had disappeared when Jeanne, at the urging of SFBC Anapharm, did not demand an autopsy.

In their search for answers, Henri's brothers and sisters turned to the media in the hopes that a journalist might find Henri's story worth investigating. Their overtures were entertained by an investigative journalist who was already preparing an exposé on the Canadian clinical trial industry and research participant safety practices for the *Fifth Estate*, the CBC News documentary program. I was interviewed by the *Fifth Estate* in relation to this exposé, and it was through this connection that I was introduced to Henri's brother Arthur.

Arthur and I had many subsequent meetings, which often included his brother Leo and his sisters Thérèse and Odile, who brought Henri to life in colourful reflection. I don't recall why the *Fifth Estate* decided not to air the exposé, but that decision paved the way for me to tell Henri's story. The information in this chapter came from recordings of the lovely and lively conversations I had with Henri's brothers and sisters and from the medical documents they permitted me to access and publicize.

If I had met Henri on the morning of September 20, 2005, perhaps he would have recounted his story to me as we sat together waiting for the ambulance to arrive. I would have listened to him intently, and I would have told him that perhaps he'd withheld certain information from the test facility because he feared that disclosing it would jeopardize his participation in the study. I would have assured Henri that he was not at fault — it was the test facility's responsibility to ensure that he understood why it was important for him to disclose his past medical history, the medications he was taking, and the effects that the study medication was having on him. I would have told him that without an understanding of the study and its ramifications, he did not have agency to make decisions about his participation. Rest in peace, Henri.

2

"WHERE DID YOU GET THAT CANOE?"

SFBC ANAPHARM BECAME A CLIENT OF OUR RESEARCH ETHICS BOARD IN 1997. AT that time, its name was simply Anapharm, and it had become a jewel of the generic drug industry.

CREATING RESEARCH NORMS WHERE NONE EXISTED

When it came to reviewing Anapharm's studies, our research ethics board established a specific quorum of members that included pharmacologists and comparative biologists, in addition to the requisite members. We met routinely with Anapharm's management to develop ethically acceptable norms particular to the company's research niche, especially where the relevant policies and guidance documents were silent. These norms included what information could and could not be used in a study advertisement to recruit research participants, what constituted reasonable compensation for a research participant's time, and the maximum amount of time a research participant could remain in the test facility (referred to as "confinement"). Anapharm was respectful of the conditions and suggestions that our research ethics board placed on its studies. It was a very open, sincere, and engaging time in our business relationship.

Anapharm had one test facility in Quebec City, and all of its studies were conducted there. In 2000, as the volume of studies it was running increased, it opened a second test facility on Decarie Boulevard in Montreal. I attended the christening of this test facility. It was a very classy and intimate affair. The provincial premier was there, as were the mayor of Montreal and representatives from Health Canada and the pharmaceutical industry. I was so proud to be part of this wonderful success story.

In March of 2002, we learned that Anapharm had been purchased by Florida-based SFBC International, Inc., a large American contract research company. This purchase made SFBC the largest early-phase contract research company in North America.[1] At first, nothing much changed at the newly named company; we interacted with the same people, and the studies submitted to our research ethics board were unremarkable. However, our feeling of reassurance quickly dissipated. SFBC Anapharm began to challenge the decisions of our research ethics board by submitting studies and documentation outside the ethically acceptable norms we had established together.

I recall a very bizarre lunch meeting with SFBC Anapharm's chief operating officer in the fall of 2004. We met at the restaurant of an airport hotel in Dorval. As soon as we'd sat down and exchanged pleasantries, my lunch partner got right to the point: She wanted my colleague Martin Letendre to be removed from any involvement in SFBC Anapharm's studies.

Martin had joined our company as the director of ethics and government affairs in 2003. Part of his role was the day-to-day administrative management of our research ethics board's operations.

Once I realized that SFBC Anapharm's chief operating officer was serious about her request, I asked her why she had made it. She told me that she feared Martin would interfere in the way SFBC Anapharm wanted to conduct its studies.

To make her point, she described a fictitious clinical trial that included a fourteen-day confinement period. She was worried that Martin would not allow SFBC Anapharm to conduct such a trial. I reminded her that Martin was an administrator, not a member of the research ethics board, and that the decision to approve this type of research would come from the members of the research ethics board and would be based on ethically acceptable norms for such studies.

The remainder of our meeting was very uncomfortable. As I passed Martin's office upon my return, he asked me how my meeting went. I said, "It went fine. She just wanted me to fire you!"

CONFINEMENT STUDIES

Within a week of this meeting, and without any prior warning or consultation, SFBC Anapharm submitted a clinical trial to our research ethics board for review that confined research participants at the test facility for fourteen days. It was immediately disapproved.

Our research ethics board's policy on confinement was derived from the conclusions of an experiment conducted by a research team led by Philip Zimbardo at Stanford University in 1971.[2] The study set out to investigate what makes a prison an unpleasant environment. More specifically, the research team wanted to know whether the prison environment becomes unpleasant because it is full of disagreeable people, or whether the prison environment itself makes the people in it disagreeable. The research team screened seventy-five men and enrolled the twenty-four who appeared the most normal and healthy, based on their psychological test scores.

One-half of the men were randomly chosen to be prison guards. They were given uniforms and told that they were to keep the prison in order. The other half of the men were randomly chosen to be prisoners, and they were to be locked in a cell for twenty-four hours a day for fourteen days. (This study design would not be approved by a research ethics board today — I hope.)

Early in the study, self-proclaimed pacifists assigned as guards began behaving sadistically. They fell into the role of remorseless disciplinarians, inflicting abuse, humiliation, and suffering on the prisoners. As the study progressed, the guards became more sadistic and created an atmosphere of terror. Prisoners became blindly obedient and allowed themselves to be dehumanized, but eventually rebelled against the guards, violently.

The two-week study was abruptly terminated after six days of confinement due to the guards' pathological behaviour and the prisoners' emotional reactions to that behaviour. The research team concluded that it was the prison environment, rather than the personality traits of the individuals participating in the simulation, that caused the participants to behave the way they did.

Our research ethics board extrapolated the conclusions of the Zimbardo study in its determination of a safe confinement period. It conjectured that, since a medical physician was available to the research participants at all times at the test facility, a seven-day confinement period would be acceptable.

STUDY ADVERTISEMENTS

Another hint that something was amiss with SFBC Anapharm came when they started to run sketchy study advertisements. On a mid-summer morning in 2005, one of my employees tapped at my office door. She told me about a study advertisement she had heard on a local Montreal radio station on her drive to work. We sat in my office and listened to the radio, waiting for the advertisement to be played again. It finally was, and it was jaw-dropping. It went something like this:

> Voice 1 (female): "Hi, Jacques! Where did you get that canoe?"
> Voice 2 (male): "Allo, Marie! I bought it with the money I made volunteering in a study at SFBC Anapharm."
> Voice 1: "Wow, Jacques. You must have made a lot of money. That's a fancy canoe!"
> Voice 2: "Yes, Marie. I did make a lot of money. You can, too."

As the advertisement continued, Jacques told Marie how easy it was to make upwards of five thousand dollars by participating in a clinical trial at SFBC Anapharm. Then he provided a phone number Marie could call for more information.

We were dumbfounded as to how this study advertisement had obtained approval from our research ethics board, since it breached the ethical norms we had established with SFBC Anapharm. In particular, a study advertisement must be written in a way that protects potential research participants from undue influence and it must not overstate the potential benefits of participation, which the promise of enough money to buy a canoe obviously did. By emphasizing Jacques's canoe, SFBC Anapharm was attempting to influence potential research participants by flaunting the monetary benefits they would receive, yet, at the same time, was concealing the potential risks of study participation to balance the benefits.

Another point of confusion was how SFBC Anapharm was able to compensate research participants up to five thousand dollars, as this was way above the maximum amount ever approved by our research ethics board. Our board had implemented a calculation for compensation of lost wages based on the average hourly rate of pay for a construction worker in Ontario. In 2005, this rate was approximately $20 per hour. For the maximum approved study confinement of seven days, a research participant would be compensated $1,120 (seven days times eight hours per day times $20 per hour), not $5,000.

We quickly assembled a team and worked double-duty to examine every document that SFBC Anapharm had submitted to our research ethics board for review over the previous year. Although we were relieved to find that our board had never approved study advertisements with controversial compensation amounts and methods, it horrified us to imagine that SFBC Anapharm was running these advertisements without ethics approval.

During our review of SFBC Anapharm's submissions, we noticed that studies that had been either disapproved or conditionally approved by our research ethics board were never revised and resubmitted for approval, as had been this client's normal practice in the past. We decided to reach out to the management of SFBC Anapharm for a heart-to-heart meeting concerning these important matters. We sent a series of emails and left numerous voice-mail messages, but we were confused and concerned when our overtures were met with deliberate attempts to obfuscate and disregard the issues.

LETICIA

We reached our crisis point on August 23, 2005, when, at around 2:00 p.m., the usual quiet of the office was suddenly interrupted by a woman screaming. Her voice appeared to be coming from an office down the hall from mine. I dropped what I was doing and ran toward the voice, only to discover that it was coming from a speakerphone. I sat down among a few co-workers who had already gathered near the telephone. I could barely comprehend what this woman was trying to tell us. She spoke quickly in between hitched breaths. Her name was Leticia and she was calling us from inside the SFBC Anapharm test facility in Montreal. After we established that she wasn't in imminent danger, we reassured her that we would do everything we could to help her.

Leticia was able to tell us that she was taking part in a clinical trial and that she had been confined in the Montreal test facility for twenty days — and still had another thirteen days to go. At seven thirty that morning, she had gone into the communal women's bathroom, where she was assaulted by another female research participant. Leticia immediately complained to the research staff, and they had reassured her that someone would come to see her. After waiting in fear for over six hours, and unable to stop crying, she called the only phone number listed on her informed consent form: the number for the research participant inquiry line of our research ethics board.

Leticia had recently immigrated to Canada and was living near Toronto. SFBC Anapharm had recruited her and about ninety other individuals from the Toronto area to participate in this and other clinical trials. She wanted us to get her out of the test facility so she could go back home to her family.

We hovered around the speaker, listening to Leticia's story and frantically writing messages to each other on small pieces of paper. We asked Leticia which study she was participating in so that we could retrieve it from our database, but she couldn't recall any of the study details. She knew only that she had to stay in the clinical trial for thirteen more days before she would receive her money.

Martin Letendre reassured Leticia of her rights as a research participant and asked her to send us her informed consent form by fax or email as soon as possible. He also told her about her legal rights and urged her to call the police, especially if she felt that she might get assaulted again. Martin then placed an urgent call to SFBC Anapharm's management, but he was told that everyone was in a meeting. He instructed the receptionist to interrupt the meeting and to tell those present that his call was urgent. No one came to the phone.

While we waited for Leticia's information, we tried to summarize what we knew: Leticia, an immigrant who lived near Toronto, was participating in a clinical trial in Montreal; the trial included a thirty-three-day confinement period; our phone number had been provided to her on her informed consent form; she had been assaulted that morning by another research participant; and she wanted us to get her home to her family. It was a lot of incredible information to process.

As we sat together, Martin received a call from SFBC Anapharm's medical director, who did not appear alarmed to hear about Leticia. He made no attempts to reassure Martin that Leticia's situation would be attended to. Instead, he guilelessly pointed out that, for reasons of confidentiality, he was not at liberty to discuss Leticia or any aspect of the study because this particular study was not under the jurisdiction of our research ethics board.

At that moment, Jacques's canoe, the compensation scheme, the long confinement periods, and the disappearing studies all made sense: SFBC Anapharm was using the services of another research ethics board to obtain approval for practices that our board deemed unethical. They were forum shopping. We continued to sit there, awestruck, for what felt like an eternity.

Forum shopping, in the context of research ethics review, is the practice of choosing a research ethics board, or forum, based on the relative ease of the review and the perception that it will result in a favourable decision. When a research study has obtained an unfavourable or conditional review, forum shopping provides the researcher a way to circumvent addressing the research ethics board's concerns by abandoning that board and selecting another board that will provide a more favourable review. Most researchers are probably unaware of how prejudicial this practice is to the rights, safety, and welfare of their research participants and to the integrity of the research study.

Leticia called us three more times that day and once the following day. SFBC Anapharm would not allow her to fax or email us her informed consent form, even though this form was her personal property and she could do whatever she wanted with it. To save time, Leticia read the form to us over the phone. Indeed, she had consented to participate in a thirty-three-day confinement study at the SFBC Anapharm test facility in Montreal. Our research ethics board's contact details were provided on the informed consent form for research participants to call should they have any questions about their rights and welfare. Yet our board wasn't listed as the research ethics board that had reviewed and approved the study.

Leticia, along with the other research participants enrolled in this clinical trial, had been bused to Montreal from Toronto and would be bused back only after completing the trial. Similarly, the compensation schedule was backloaded — that is, the participants would be paid only upon completion of the entire clinical trial. Both of these practices were unethical.

We don't know what happened to Leticia, and now that almost two decades have passed, we probably never will. One can assume that she never participated in a clinical trial again and that her trust in the clinical research industry was forever damaged.

HEALTHY VOLUNTEERS

SFBC Anapharm recruited "healthy volunteers" from the general population to participate in its clinical trials. The term "healthy volunteer" is commonly used in the clinical research world to refer to a research participant who does not present with or have a history of significant physical or psychological health problems. But is this a sound description?

The World Health Organization (WHO) defines "health" as "a state of complete physical, mental and social well-being and not merely the absence of disease or infirmity."[3] This definition has not been revised by WHO for seventy-five years. Health Canada defines a "healthy life" as "making positive choices that enhance your personal physical, mental and spiritual health."[4] If we were to combine these two definitions and include one's emotional well-being, we could arrive at the following definition for the term "healthy": a state of complete physical, mental, social, spiritual, and emotional well-being, and not merely the absence of disease or infirmity. Most people equate the state of being healthy with the physical dimensions of health and think of it as the absence of disease or infirmity. Others may include the mental aspects of health in their definition, but very few consider the effects of social, spiritual, and emotional factors on an individual's state of health.

To be considered "healthy" by SFBC Anapharm, an individual had to successfully pass a screening assessment prior to study enrolment. The screening did not assess the individual's mental, spiritual, or social well-being, and it was only in the medical history section that potential participants were asked to divulge their psychiatric past. One wonders how many faithfully did.

The individual who attacked Leticia in the women's bathroom on the morning of August 23, 2005, could have appeared "healthy" upon screening, but without undertaking a prior, objective assessment of her mental or social well-being, SFBC Anapharm was derelict in its duty to protect Leticia and other participants from harm. Additionally, the mental health effects of a thirty-three-day confinement period on the participants should have been monitored carefully by SFBC Anapharm. At one point in our relationship with SFBC Anapharm, our research ethics board recommended that a psychiatrist or psychologist be present during the seven-day confinement periods, but SFBC Anapharm refused such intervention because it would add to the cost of the study.

The subjectivity associated with the word "healthy" precludes it from accurately describing non-diseased research participants. Similarly, the word "volunteer" cannot be used as a descriptor, since almost all definitions of the word include the performance of a service or other undertaking willingly and without being paid. The term "research participant" is the only way to describe the contribution to research made by individuals who, by virtue of their agency and decision-making power, voluntarily consent to participate in research.

RECALL

The only benefit research participants at SFBC Anapharm expected to receive for participating in a study was money. And as we learned from Leticia and many other research participants, it was usually the only detail of the study they could recall. To explain this, we need to explore the results of studies that have examined this phenomenon.

One such study was conducted in 2008 to determine which elements of a thirteen-page informed consent form were recalled by research participants.[5] Variables such as sex, age, and education level were carefully controlled in this study; in fact, 90 percent of the individuals had a university degree, and 60 percent were medical students. After confirming that they were ready to provide their consent, each of the eighty-two individuals was asked to complete a six-item questionnaire to test their recall of what they were consenting to. Of the twenty-three risks mentioned in the informed consent form, the highest number recalled was six, and this was by only two research participants. Yet all the individuals except one (98.8 percent) could recall the exact value of the study compensation. Why was information concerning compensation retained more successfully when the other study information was not?

In his book *The Tipping Point: How Little Things Can Make a Big Difference*, Canadian journalist and author Malcolm Gladwell introduced the concept of the "stickiness factor" and discussed how it affects our ability to remember things. Gladwell described how the television shows *Sesame Street* and *Blue's Clues* restructured their educational content to create memorable messages for their young viewers. They achieved this through researching the behaviour and viewing habits of children who watched their shows and then modifying segments of their shows based on what they had learned from their research. Then they repeated the research and modified segments, over and over again. The researchers concluded that for a message to be sticky, it must be easily understood, repeated a number of times, and presented in a logical order. They also found that children were more likely to recall a message when they were actively involved in its evolution.

In the recall study, the individuals were able to retain information concerning their compensation because it was stickier — that is, it was presented in a manner that was relatable and easy to understand compared to the other key details of the study. Imagine what the individuals would be able to recall if researchers employed methods such as interactive study information sessions to make other study-related information stickier. If this were done, individuals would gain the knowledge they needed to make an informed decision about their participation before and during the study.

END OF AN ERA

At some point during the incident with Leticia, Martin requested that SFBC Anapharm grant us permission to conduct an audit at the test facility. The company flatly denied the request. Then we requested an urgent meeting with SFBC Anapharm's management. That was also denied. So, with the blessing of our research ethics board, we ceased all review activity associated with SFBC Anapharm's clinical trials until they agreed to meet with us.

It took over a week, but SFBC Anapharm finally agreed to a meeting at the test facility on the morning of Tuesday, September 20, 2005. We sat in an us-and-them pattern around an oval table in a chilly, nondescript conference room. I attempted to break the silence by reminding the SFBC Anapharm folks of why we were there, but before I could get my words out, the chief operating officer interrupted me and took control of the narrative. This changed the entire tone of the meeting and placed us in a defensive position.

About forty-five minutes into the meeting, as the back-and-forth was becoming nauseating, it became clear that SFBC Anapharm did not appreciate the rigour of our research ethics board reviews and instead requested they be more lax. We were presented with a "win-win" scenario: Our research ethics board would relax various criteria in order to approve the studies, and SFBC Anapharm would then have no reason to seek alternative ethics review boards. I remember how dispirited I felt at that moment. I sat there stoically, trying to find words to hide my emotions, but all that came out was a request for a fifteen-minute break to speak privately with our group.

With the SFBC Anapharm team out of the room, I appealed to our team to terminate our relationship with the company immediately. I envisioned a scenario where SFBC Anapharm involved itself in a situation that could potentially harm research participants and its inaction to prevent such harm could be catastrophic. I explained that we had an opportunity to remove ourselves from any association with SFBC Anapharm before such a situation would occur.

It was a difficult discussion, but we all agreed to end the meeting with an announcement that we were terminating our agreement to provide ethics review services. No one from the SFBC Anapharm team reacted to our decision. We said our goodbyes as pleasantly as we could and drove back to the office. It didn't take long for me to start second-guessing our decision, given the importance of SFBC Anapharm's studies to the viability of our business. But I would soon learn that it was one of the smartest decisions we ever made.

On September 23, our research ethics board chair, Dr. Barry Brown, sent a formal letter of termination to SFBC Anapharm. In the letter, Dr. Brown explained that forum shopping for research ethics board approval raised serious ethical and legal issues for all parties. He specified that by seeking approval from another research ethics board in order to bypass mandatory and stringent ethical requirements, SFBC Anapharm was jeopardizing the general safety and well-being of its research participants. Dr. Brown added that the judgment of our research ethics board members must not be impeded by commercial imperatives and this was why forum shopping must be proscribed.

Dr. Brown provided SFBC Anapharm thirty days to transfer all of its studies under our research ethics board's jurisdiction to another board, as required by Health Canada. Shortly thereafter, we received a letter from the attorneys of SFBC Anapharm demanding that our research ethics board lift its suspension and resume its services. They gave our research ethics board ten days to accomplish this; otherwise, they would launch a lawsuit.

Those ten days came and went, and on November 3 we terminated all of our services to SFBC Anapharm. We were never sued by SFBC Anapharm. It was an abrupt and disturbing end to a hopeful era.

HEALTH CANADA

By this time, various events like those described in this and the preceding chapter had made their way to a popular Canadian email platform for research ethics. Members of this forum supported sending a formal request to Health Canada to inspect SFBC Anapharm's research practices. At the end of December 2005, a group of us emailed a letter to Jean St-Pierre at the Health Products and Food Branch Inspectorate of Health Canada. A copy of the letter was sent to the director general of the Therapeutic Products Directorate (now known as the Pharmaceutical Drugs Directorate) and the auditor general of Canada. However, we purposely omitted the name of SFBC Anapharm from the letter since it was threatening to sue us if we disclosed its behaviour.

Our message to Jean St-Pierre was clear: How did Health Canada expect our research ethics board to fulfill its duties if researchers were not being held accountable for neglecting to protect the rights, safety, and welfare of research participants? In the letter, we cited the following recent examples of the test facility's aberrant behaviour and negligence:

- the practice of forum shopping for studies involving situations or study drugs that our research ethics board had previously placed stringent and mandatory conditions on (such as extended confinement periods)
- failure to respect a research participant's request to withdraw from a study, failure to provide a safe confinement environment, and failure to properly address a research participant's complaint
- failure to allow our research ethics board access to monitor the conduct at the test facility
- use of a recruitment campaign that violated the ethical principles of human research and compromised the ability of a research participant to provide free and informed consent to participate in the research
- lack of co-operation in the evaluation of a research participant's suspicious, sudden death

- use of our research ethics board's name and telephone number on informed consent forms for
  studies that were not under its auspices

Jean St-Pierre replied immediately to our letter. In his email he noted that the issues we raised surrounding the rights, safety, and welfare of research participants were "serious issues and must be addressed in a timely manner." His formal reply to our letter was not issued until February 8, 2006. We will return to his response in chapter 5.

3

ETHICS FOR SALE

THE IMPOSTER COMPANY

When I first established my research company in 1992, I spent a lot of my time visiting pharmaceutical companies in Quebec and Ontario, trying to sell them on the idea of using a contract research company. There were only a few companies like mine operating in Canada at the time. I felt that I carried the burden of creating the market I wanted to compete in.

I visited SmithKline Beecham in Mississauga in the summer of 1993. My meeting was in the early afternoon, which meant that I had to leave Montreal, by car, in the early morning. I was just scraping by in those formative years, so to portray the image of a successful business owner, I hid my car behind a building near SmithKline Beecham and entered the company as if I had just gotten out of a taxi from the airport. Fake it until you make it.

I greeted the receptionist with my business card, and while I was telling her whom I was there to visit, she gestured for me to complete the sign-in sheet, as if I should have known that this was standard practice. The sign-in sheet was clipped to a board at the reception desk, and a pen hung from the board by a metal ball chain, like the ones we used to see in banks. I had to pull the chain taut to write, being careful not to snap it from the clipboard.

I entered my information in the first empty row under all of the other visitor data, at the bottom of the page: the date and time of my arrival, my full name, the company I was with, and whom I was at SmithKline Beecham to see. As I wrote out my company's name, my gaze locked on the row of data above mine. There, in that little paper cell, someone had written my company's name. I glanced to the left and quickly memorized the first and last name of the person behind the entry and the time of his arrival. The imposter had not signed out yet, so was still in the building.

I sat down in the leather reception chair and frantically transcribed to paper the imposter company's information before I lost it from my short-term memory. My hand was shaking, and I feared I wouldn't be able to read my own handwriting. When I calmed down, I rewrote the note to myself.

In those days, my father was also my company's lawyer. Many times during our interactions I wondered where our father-daughter relationship ended and where our lawyer-client relationship began. For my father, it was probably a delicate balancing act, seeing past his little girl to the grown businesswoman she had become.

During my meeting at SmithKline Beecham that afternoon, I couldn't stop thinking about John, my father-lawyer. When we had incorporated my company, did he have the objectivity to do a proper name search and ensure that other measures were taken to protect my company properly? These thoughts hijacked my meeting, and I struggled to focus on why I was there. As I walked out of the reception area after the meeting, the receptionist gestured for me to sign out. This gave me another opportunity to verify the imposter company's information, and I saw that the man representing it had departed the building thirty minutes earlier.

By the time I was able to call John, I must have convinced myself that he was at fault for the corporate name confusion, because he said that my tone was accusatory. I apologized, embarrassed. John promised to look into the details of my company's incorporation and get back to me. A day or two later, he called to assure me that his law firm had done a thorough name search prior to filing the incorporation papers. He sent me the search results that his articling student had obtained from the registrar's office. The results were clear; no one in Canada was using the corporate name at the time I was proposing it for my new company.

John went into full sleuth mode and discovered some interesting information about the imposter company. The first revelation was the reassuring fact that it was neither incorporated nor registered, which supported the results of the name search. The company was in the business of market access. Its main service was to lobby provincial governments to include specific drugs and devices on the lists of products they would cover on their health plans. The company's clients included pharmaceutical and medical device companies in Canada.

John's legal opinion was that, even though the imposter company was not involved in clinical research, both companies serviced the same Canadian industry and our common name had the potential to cause confusion. So he sent the imposter company a cease-and-desist letter.

The imposter company fought hard to convince John that it deserved to keep the name, but its arguments were not supported by the law. Two principals of the company told John that they would visit me in Montreal to work on a solution. John advised me to listen to their arguments but to remain confident in the knowledge that the law was on my side.

SHHHHH! A MAN IS SPEAKING

Within a few weeks, the two principals of the imposter company, Jack Corman and Gregory Glenn, visited me at my office in Montreal. During our brief meeting, even though I sat in the power chair, the men seized the opportunity to criticize my sex, youth, and inexperience. They spoke to me in what would become a familiar tone, one that I would hear throughout my career.

The men predicted that my business was doomed to fail. They cited what they said were proven statistics that most female-owned companies folded in their first three years. They contended that it would be easier for me to find a new corporate name, given the inevitable demise of my company. When that argument failed to impress me, they maintained that they had no intention whatsoever to offer services within the clinical research space, and therefore the potential for confusion was negligible, or non-existent. At one point near the end of our meeting, the two men even offered to reimburse the costs of replacing all my company stationery if I agreed to change the name. This must have been where the term "manspeak" was born.

I don't recall getting upset at this meeting or engaging in negotiations. I stood my ground, and the men had no other choice but to find another name for their company. The flames of my determination as a woman in business were certainly fanned at this meeting.

Given our unconnected business pursuits, I never thought I would encounter either of these men again. But life is full of surprises.

JACK OF ALL TRADES

In the mid- to late 1990s, drug companies and other private research sponsors began migrating their studies from public settings, like hospitals and universities, to physicians practising medicine in the community. Our research ethics board began operating in 1995, and most of its clients at that time consisted of these community-based researchers, as they did not have direct access to hospital or university research ethics boards.

Our research ethics board was instantly embraced by the market. It filled a specific need with high-quality, rigorous ethics review services and operated across the country in both official languages. Its success did not go unnoticed by a competitor operating out of the Toronto area, IRB Services. The owner of this private research ethics board was none other than Jack Corman — the same Jack Corman who, less than two years earlier, had promised he had no intention of working in the clinical research space.

For the most part, our two research ethics boards operated in the Canadian market without tripping over each other. The market was new and growing as more and more community-based researchers emerged. IRB Services would attempt to provoke us from time to time, but we always understood these irritants to be part of healthy competition.

Things got a little dicey when IRB Services added Google Ads to its competition salvo. Google Ads is a pay-per-click platform often used by organizations in marketing campaigns. When someone uses Google to look for products or services, it displays a series of results that match their search. Behind the scenes, advertisers normally use two methods to boost their rankings in a Google search. One is search engine optimization, or SEO, which involves improving a website to increase its visibility to internet search engines. The other is Google Ads, which allows an advertiser to bid on keywords that best describe its products or services. The advertiser agrees to pay Google when a user clicks on its advertisement as a result of a search. Most advertisers set a daily pay limit within their advertising budgets. Google enters all the keywords it deems relevant to a particular search into the auction and gives each advertiser a quality score from one to ten, based on its relevance to the search query keywords. Google then gives each advertisement an ad rank score by multiplying the advertiser's quality score by its maximum bid. The ads with the highest ad rank scores are the ones that show up first in the search results.

IRB Services was using Google Ads as part of its advertising campaign. Among its Google Ads keywords was our corporate name. So whenever anyone searched for our research ethics board using Google, an ad for IRB Services would pop up in their search results, potentially driving business to IRB Services instead of us.

We asked IRB Services to stop using our corporate name. Our request was ignored, so we decided to work it out another way. Each morning, before the workday started, we searched our corporate name using Google, and every time IRB Services' advertisement came up, we clicked it. We repeated this over and over until its daily pay limit was reached. Within days, IRB Services stopped using our corporate name in its Google Ads campaign.

FORUM SELLING

One advantage that our research ethics board had over IRB Services was that it was able to offer services in French. Our client base included community-based researchers in pockets of Quebec, like Rivière-du-Loup and Thetford Mines, that were often overlooked by clinical trial sponsors. We nurtured these relationships over a decade, not because of the volume of studies they conducted, but to offer the patients of these community-based researchers access to clinical trials.

One can imagine how distressing it was when we realized that many of these researchers had stopped submitting their studies to our research ethics board in favour of IRB Services. When we questioned them about their change of heart, they all told the same story, that IRB Services offered them a faster review at a lower price. IRB Services was engaging in forum selling, a questionable and insidious practice in which a company reduces its review times and prices in order to be awarded more research reviews. IRB Services pitched its quick and low-cost reviews under the slogan "Real Reviews in Real Time," and a portion of our clients were dazzled by it.

It remains a mystery how IRB Services knew that these Quebec researchers were our clients. One theory involves an ex-employee of ours who had direct access to our research ethics board's client list. When this employee left our company under acrimonious circumstances around 2003, she threatened to "sell" our client list to IRB Services. It was shortly after this that the francophone researchers began receiving calls from IRB Services. When I confronted IRB Services about this, Jack Corman responded, "Honestly, I have absolutely no knowledge that anyone here received your client list, nor has ever seen it." Without any direct evidence to the contrary, I had to take him at his word.

Operators of a research ethics board have a duty to ensure that its members have the expertise, independence, and multidisciplinary background essential for a competent ethical review of the research under its auspices. They must also ensure that their members have sufficient time and resources to conduct these reviews. To attract and retain qualified research ethics board members such as physicians, lawyers, and pharmacologists, it is important that they are compensated for their time in accordance with their professions. Reducing our prices to compete with IRB Services would have meant skimping on board members' compensation or using less qualified members. Similarly, we couldn't reduce our turnaround time, as it was already very tight. Board members received the study documents for review one week prior to meeting together to determine the outcome. Reducing their compensation or shortening their time for review were both very risky actions that could impact the rigour and quality of the review and affect the rights, safety, and welfare of research participants. Neither of these changes was an option for us.

FORUM SHOPPING

IRB Services, perhaps inadvertently, produced an environment in which its forum selling led to forum shopping. It didn't take long for the company to gain a reputation within the clinical research community for its lenient reviews and lower prices. Many of our clients liked this type of service and flocked to IRB Services for their ethics review needs. For some clients that remained, the option to move to IRB Services gave them confidence to challenge conditions that our research ethics board placed on their studies. We heard statements like "Jack would approve this study without these conditions!" and "Jack told me that your conditions are ridiculous!" Although we made Health Canada aware of what was happening, the agency made no attempts to stop this dangerous and unethical practice.

As noted in the previous chapter, forum selling eventually spread to SFBC Anapharm, our research ethics board's biggest client at that time. IRB Services' initial attempts to charm SFBC Anapharm were unsuccessful since it couldn't compete with our board's decade of experience in perfecting its reviews for this client. But IRB Services did succeed in casting doubt on our board's expertise concerning certain types of studies. SFBC Anapharm began submitting studies that our research ethics board had placed conditions on or had ethical concerns with to IRB Services. Although we didn't know it at the time, forum shopping eventually eroded our relationship with SFBC Anapharm, a relationship that relied on trust and good faith.

WHAT COULD POSSIBLY GO WRONG?

Many situations can render an individual vulnerable. For example, someone who uses a wheelchair is not considered vulnerable until they are placed in a situation that makes them so, such as being confronted with an out-of-service elevator in their apartment building.

Participating in a research study has the potential to trigger a state of vulnerability if it places research participants in a situation where they are susceptible to harm. Consider a study investigating the social impacts of domestic violence in which participants are required to complete a questionnaire about a past incident of emotional, physical, or sexual victimization. Reliving such a horrific experience could place a participant in a situation of vulnerability, so it is incumbent on researchers to anticipate such harms and make participants aware that referrals to support services or other safety protections will be available to them.

Forum shopping allowed SFBC Anapharm to engage in clinical trials that our research ethics board had prohibited due to its concerns for the research participants. SFBC Anapharm could direct high-risk clinical trials, such as those with extended confinement periods, to IRB Services for review. Forum shopping also gave SFBC Anapharm the green light to employ unethical recruitment advertisements and compensation schemes. IRB Services enabled SFBC Anapharm's deceptive practices, and together they created a situation of vulnerability for financially disadvantaged research participants.

As I described in previous chapters, Henri and Leticia were both financially disadvantaged. The only reasonable motivation for them to participate in clinical trials was their desperate need for money. Because they were lured by large payouts, the judgment critical for them to weigh the studies' potential risks was clouded. Their consent to participate was unduly influenced, and they lacked the knowledge they needed to ensure that their consent was informed. The resulting power imbalance created situations of vulnerability for Henri and Leticia, from which the eventual harms emerged.

Baited by SFBC Anapharm's recruitment advertisements, Henri was vulnerable to manipulation by the study staff. He feared that his compensation would be threatened if he disclosed the medications he was taking or how he was feeling. He feared being removed from the study.

In the case of Leticia, the lure of the advertised payout motivated her to participate in a clinical trial that required her to travel by bus from Toronto to Montreal in the heat of summer and subject herself to a thirty-three-day incarceration. Her payout was conditional on her completing the entire study; this unethical practice is referred to as "backloading" study compensation. Like Henri, Leticia ended up in a situation that made her vulnerable to manipulation by the study staff at the test facility.

Neither SFBC Anapharm nor IRB Services made any attempts to remedy these harms. Research participants like Henri and Leticia lacked agency, and SFBC Anapharm exploited this power imbalance by implementing manipulative tactics.

SEPTEMBER 20, 2005

September 20, 2005, will always stand out in my memory. It was the day we assembled at SFBC Anapharm's Montreal facility to confront the company about its dubious practices, including its heartbreaking treatment of Leticia. It was also the day that Henri died. And, although we would not be made aware of it for another three months, it was one day after SFBC Anapharm cancelled a clinical trial because it was in the middle of a tuberculosis outbreak.

This outbreak, which is the topic of the next chapter, was the result of the most blatant and historic case of forum shopping. The victims of this wholly preventable tragedy included nine research participants and eleven members of SFBC Anapharm's research staff, some of whom sat directly across from us at our meeting that day without so much as a precautionary word that they might have been exposed to the highly infectious bacteria.

4

"WHAT'S A FEW GRAND TO PROTECT YOUR REPUTATION?"

A RARE OUTBREAK OF TUBERCULOSIS

We spent most of the morning and early afternoon of December 15, 2005, gathering names for our holiday card and gift lists and making the final arrangements for our office celebration. It was a welcome reprieve from our usual work, and employees seemed exceptionally giddy and animated. It was my favourite time of year, a time when people seemed kinder and more engaging.

The wonder of the day was abruptly hijacked by a news article posted on the research ethics email platform. It was written by David Evans, an investigative journalist from *Bloomberg News*, and it revealed the details of a tuberculosis outbreak at the SFBC Anapharm test facility in Montreal a few months earlier that had affected research participants and members of the study staff.[1] (Those in our field would eventually refer to this as the Evans Report.)

The day was transformed into a whirlwind of chaos and stress as we grappled with the details of the tragedy. From the Evans

Report, we learned that the outbreak had occurred in a clinical trial sponsored by an Edmonton-based biotechnology company called Isotechnika. The drug under investigation was ISA 247. The drug name rang a bell for some members of our team, prompting a records search to determine if our research ethics board was in any way culpable for the outbreak. We found three ISA 247 studies approved by our research ethics board in 2004, and all of them had been submitted by SFBC Anapharm. It comforted us to discover that these studies had concluded without incident in 2004 and therefore could not have been responsible for the recent outbreak. With calmer eyes, we carefully reviewed the Evans Report and saw that ground zero of the outbreak was a clinical trial approved by IRB Services. Our relief about our own involvement quickly turned to anger and frustration. Forum shopping had, once again, led to harm.

TUBERCULOSIS

To appreciate the issues at the heart of the Montreal tuberculosis outbreak, it may help to know a bit about how tuberculosis spreads. Tuberculosis is an airborne disease caused by the slow-growing bacterium *Mycobacterium tuberculosis*, which is spread when a person with the untreated disease in their lungs coughs, sneezes, or even laughs or sings. Exposure to the bacterium does not always result in tuberculosis disease. When most people breathe the bacterium into their lungs, their body mounts an immune response against it and prevents it from multiplying. However, the body doesn't kill the bacterium; it remains in the body in a dormant state called latent tuberculosis infection. In order to kill the bacterium, the infected individual must commit to a long-term course of antibiotics.

People with latent tuberculosis infection are asymptomatic and cannot infect others. Most remain disease-free for their entire lives. But if the infection is not treated and if the infected person's immune system becomes weak or compromised by drugs, diseases, or other conditions, the bacteria can become active and multiply over a period of weeks or months, resulting in tuberculosis disease.

People with tuberculosis disease are symptomatic. They may have a severe cough for three weeks or longer and may be coughing up blood or sputum. They may also have chest pain and feel weak or tired. They may experience chills, fever, and night sweats. They may lose weight and have little to no appetite. The chest x-ray of someone with tuberculosis disease is abnormal compared to that of someone with latent tuberculosis infection.

Latent tuberculosis infection and tuberculosis disease have two things in common: They can be diagnosed by a simple blood or skin test, and they require long-term treatment with antibiotics. In one test for tuberculosis, a small amount of tuberculin is injected under the top layer of skin on the inner forearm. Tuberculin is a mixture of non-infectious proteins derived from *Mycobacterium tuberculosis*. People who have previously been exposed to the bacterium will have a positive tuberculin skin test, characterized by a firm, red bump at the tuberculin injection site that develops within two or three days of the injection. A positive tuberculin skin test cannot tell how long a person has been infected with the bacterium or distinguish between latent tuberculosis infection and tuberculosis disease. Further tests have to be performed to confirm the diagnosis.

Back in 1984, when I was beginning my Ph.D. research project, I had to have a tuberculin skin test. My lab was situated in the University of Alberta Hospital, and it was the hospital's responsibility to ensure that I didn't pose an infectious threat to patients. The test took less than five minutes to administer, was painless, and did not prevent me from going on with the rest of my day. My test was negative, meaning that I had never been exposed to the bacterium, and I was allowed to begin working in the hospital lab after the results came in.

PREVENTING THE PERFECT STORM

SFBC Anapharm was studying ISA 247, an investigational drug that belongs to a drug class called calcineurin inhibitors. Drugs in this class, such as cyclosporine A, are immunosuppressants. They inhibit the body's immune system, reducing its ability to defend the body against diseases. ISA 247 was a new candidate in this drug class. Early-phase clinical trials had demonstrated that it was as effective as the other drugs in its class, but its full toxicity profile, including heart toxicity, had not yet been established.

Under normal body conditions, a suppressed immune system would be very dangerous. However, when someone receives a transplanted organ, such as a kidney, heart, or lung, the body sees the organ as something foreign and mounts an immune response against it. By trying to protect the body, the immune system promotes the body's rejection of the transplanted organ. Therefore, immunosuppressants are commonly used to prevent the rejection of transplanted organs. They are also used to treat psoriasis and rheumatoid arthritis. In these diseases immunosuppressants slow the overreactive immune system and prevent it from causing damage to the body's own tissues.

Given that clinical trials of ISA 247 had the potential to compromise the research participants' immune systems and included confinement periods of various durations, it was important that participants were protected from exposure to anyone with an active infection. Our research ethics board insisted on testing for infectious diseases such as HIV, tuberculosis, and hepatitis B and C and excluding individuals with current infections from participating. It was equally important to ensure that anyone with latent tuberculosis infection was excluded because ISA 247 could weaken their immune system over time, providing an environment for the bacteria to activate and multiply, resulting in tuberculosis disease. Therefore, people who had recently travelled to a country where tuberculosis was endemic were excluded since they might have been exposed to someone with tuberculosis disease and then developed latent tuberculosis infection.

These conditions were clearly communicated to SFBC Anapharm. Before enroling a potential research participant into any of the ISA 247 studies approved by our research ethics board, it was necessary for the test facility to

- conduct a thorough history to exclude individuals who had recently travelled to a tuberculosis endemic country,
- perform a physical examination to rule out individuals with signs and symptoms of active infection,
- test for infectious diseases such as HIV and hepatitis B and C to rule out individuals with active infections, and
- test for tuberculosis to rule out individuals with latent tuberculosis infection or tuberculosis disease.

CHRONOLOGY OF EVENTS

To create a timeline of events related to the tuberculosis outbreak, I combined information from the Evans Report with that of two other reports. One aired on CBC/Radio-Canada's *Enquête*, the French version of the *Fifth Estate*, three years after the outbreak occurred.[2] This excellent and thoughtful account reported on the outbreak from the perspective of the injured research participants. The other is *Maclean's* magazine's 2009 exposé of the early-phase clinical trial industry in Quebec, which included some details of the tuberculosis outbreak.[3]

The events leading up to the tuberculosis outbreak are tabulated below.

Date	Day	Events
Prior to August 29, 2005		IRB Services reviewed and approved the ISA 247 study. Potential research participants were screened for participation in the clinical trial.
August 29	0	Twenty previously screened research participants (75 percent from South America, Africa, the Middle East, or Haiti) arrived at the test facility in Montreal to begin the study's first confinement period, which would last eight days. Mohsen, a participant from Kuwait, was placed in a room with Baptiste (a pseudonym), a participant from Haiti.
August 30	1	Mohsen noticed that Baptiste appeared to be sick. The first dose of ISA 247 was administered to the research participants.
September 1	3	Mohsen reported to the study staff that Baptiste was spending most of the time in bed and was lethargic, shivering, shaking, and coughing up blood. Mohsen requested to be moved to another room. Research participants noticed that the study staff seemed agitated. Baptiste was examined by SFBC Anapharm's medical director for thirty minutes in the middle of the night and then brought back to the room he shared with Mohsen.

Date	Day	Events
September 2	4	Mohsen disclosed to the other research participants that Baptiste was very sick and coughing up blood. The participants were worried that Baptiste's illness was a side effect of ISA 247. A member of the study staff assured Mohsen that Baptiste was not sick. According to Mohsen, Baptiste's condition got worse.
September 3	5	According to Isotechnika, the maker of ISA 247, SFBC Anapharm informed Isotechnika that a research participant in the trial had tuberculosis disease.
September 4	6	Baptiste was transferred to another room and isolated from Mohsen and the other research participants.
September 6	8	All research participants were sent home at the end of the first confinement period. They were told to return to the test facility for the second scheduled confinement period in two weeks.
September 19	21	The research participants returned for the second confinement period. They were herded into a meeting room and informed that the clinical trial had been cancelled because of a suspected case of tuberculosis. They were told they needed to be tested for tuberculosis and treated with a nine-month course of antibiotics if they tested positive. They were paid $6,800, the full amount of the study compensation.

UNCONSCIONABLE COMPENSATION SCHEME

The clinical trial, before it was cancelled, was to include five confinement periods totalling thirty-one days over a ten-week period. Research participants would be compensated for their participation according to the following backloaded compensation scheme:

After first confinement period	$ 200
After second confinement period	$ 300
After third confinement period	$ 400
After fourth confinement period	$ 500
After fifth confinement period	$5,400
Total compensation	$6,800

Backloaded compensation schemes are unethical because they unduly influence research participants to complete a clinical trial, and they undermine participants' rights to withdraw at any time and for any reason. Research participants experiencing a physical, emotional, or psychological injury are most affected by such schemes. For example, Leticia, the research participant we met in chapter 2, experienced a study injury on day twenty of a thirty-three-day confinement period at the SFBC Anapharm Montreal test facility. Her right to withdraw from the clinical trial was seriously impacted by the knowledge that she would be compensated for her participation only if she stayed for the remaining thirteen days.

The informed consent form that the research participants signed before participating in the ISA 247 clinical trial was approved by IRB Services' research ethics board, despite the fact that it unabashedly contained the unethical backloaded compensation scheme. IRB Services' president, Jack Corman, remarked to David Evans that study payments are often backloaded to discourage research participants from dropping out of the studies.

MONEY OVERSHADOWED THE POTENTIAL RISKS

For most of the research participants in the ISA 247 study, the total compensation amount of $6,800 seemed to be the only thing they could recall from the informed consent form. In chapter 2 I described Malcolm Gladwell's concept of the stickiness factor. For the research participants, the compensation amount was sticky. In other words, they were lured into the clinical trial by the sheer size of the compensation. This blinded them to important information on the informed consent form concerning their rights, safety, and welfare. As one participant, who ended up testing positive for tuberculosis, remarked to *Enquête*, "In my case, I was blinded by money. I am a student who earns approximately seven hundred dollars per month. When I find almost seven thousand dollars on the one hand, and I'm told that you won't die or become disabled on the other hand, then that's what I was looking for. Personally, as I told you, the fact that I was blinded by the money, I completely missed the detail that it was an immunosuppressant" (English translation of the original French quotation).

LACK OF OVERSIGHT

The Evans Report revealed that the informed consent form provided to the research participants did not list heart damage as a potential risk of the study. This was disturbing. The objective of the study was to determine the effects of ISA 247 on the heart. Heart damage was the unknown risk. There would be no reason to conduct the clinical trial if Isotechnika already had data to support that ISA 247 did not damage the heart. Therefore, it was essential to include heart damage on the informed consent form as a potential risk. The risk of tuberculosis was also missing from the informed consent form.

IRB Services approved both the screening and study protocols. These are the documents that SFBC Anapharm was required to comply with in order to properly conduct the clinical trial. It was the legal responsibility of the study sponsor, Isotechnika, to ensure that SFBC Anapharm conducted the study according to the study protocol. In the Evans Report, Isotechnika's chief operating officer remarked that Isotechnika had requested that SFBC Anapharm properly execute the infectious disease screening. He said, "You leave a lot in the hands of the people at SFBC. They have a responsibility to carry out the trial the way the sponsor asked." One is led to assume by this statement that Isotechnika failed to oversee the conduct of SFBC Anapharm to ensure that the tests were done.

BAPTISTE

From the Evans Report we know that 75 percent of the research participants in the ISA 247 study arrived in Canada from South America, Africa, the Middle East, or Haiti. In 2005, tuberculosis was endemic in parts of these areas, or present to a greater extent than in other countries or regions. Given the makeup of the ISA 247 study population, SFBC Anapharm had a duty to test each potential research participant for tuberculosis prior to enroling them in the study. Instead, it chose to simply ask the potential participants if they had recently visited any countries where tuberculosis was endemic.

The Evans Report claimed that it was the decision of both IRB Services and SFBC Anapharm to exclude the administration of the tuberculin skin test. From Evans's interview with Jack Corman, we learned that IRB Services had decided against administering the tuberculin skin test because it would have excluded too many potential research participants from the study, due to the large Haitian population in Montreal. Corman said, "It's clear the test has no utility." Too many positive tests for tuberculosis would have been costly for SFBC Anapharm and would have negatively impacted its ability to enrol the requisite number of research participants in a short period of time. So they decided to roll the dice.

Research participant number eight was a man from Haiti, a country with the highest incidence of tuberculosis in North America. Since the man's name was never disclosed in any of the reports about the outbreak, I have named him Baptiste. Mohsen was Baptiste's roommate during the ISA 247 clinical trial. Mohsen was neither a physician nor a researcher, yet even he could see that Baptiste was sick from the first day of the clinical trial.

Mohsen reported Baptiste's unhealthy condition to the study staff within the first seventy-two hours of the study. He noted that Baptiste was coughing up blood, was lethargic, and spent most of his time in bed. SFBC Anapharm's medical director examined Baptiste for thirty minutes late in the night of day 3 of the study. Mohsen told David Evans that he requested to be moved from the one-hundred-square-foot room he shared with Baptiste to another room, but the study staff denied his request, stating that there was nothing wrong with Baptiste.

Isotechnika's chief operating officer told Evans that SFBC Anapharm contacted Isotechnika on September 3, the fifth day of the study, and disclosed that one of the research participants had tuberculosis disease. As we'll see in the next chapter, this contrasts with documents filed by SFBC Anapharm stating that it first learned of Baptiste's tuberculosis disease diagnosis on September 15. Isotechnika allegedly reported the event to Health Canada on September 20.

WAIVERS OF LIABILITY

On day 8 of the study, all of the research participants were sent home without a warning that they might have been exposed to an individual with tuberculosis disease. This information was withheld from them for another thirteen days. On day 21, when they returned to the test facility for what they thought would be the start of their second eight-day confinement period, the research participants were told that the clinical trial had been cancelled and that they might have been exposed to an individual with tuberculosis disease. Mohsen told Evans that SFBC Anapharm's medical director placed the blame for the tuberculosis outbreak on Baptiste.

Most of the research participants in the ISA 247 study and approximately one hundred SFBC Anapharm study staff were tested for tuberculosis. Mohsen recalled that he was tested for tuberculosis by SFBC Anapharm in early November 2005, over two months after the outbreak. The test results revealed that nine research participants and eleven study staff had latent tuberculosis infection. Mohsen was one of them. The participants who tested positive received this news from SFBC Anapharm's medical director, who instructed them to seek a nine-month course of antibiotic treatment. It is not clear from any of the reports what the fate of Baptiste was or if he was ever sent to a hospital to receive proper medical care.

SFBC Anapharm asked the research participants to sign a waiver promising not to sue the company for damages they had suffered or might suffer in the future as a result of the clinical trial. SFBC Anapharm also requested that any research participants who did not agree to take a nine-month course of antibiotics sign another waiver giving up their rights to any further compensation from SFBC Anapharm. As quoted in the Evans Report, the waiver stated, "The volunteer hereby grants Anapharm a full, complete and final release from any and all past, present or future claim he may have."

Both of these waivers were unethical. SFBC Anapharm should have done the exact opposite; it should have offered to pay the research participants for any current and future health-care costs associated with their participation in the study. Jack Corman told Evans that he would have advised SFBC Anapharm to offer more compensation to the research participants who tested positive for tuberculosis, since they were subjected to inconvenience and possible long-term risks of developing tuberculosis disease. He added, "What's a few grand to protect your reputation?"

OCCAM'S RAZOR

SFBC Anapharm quickly deflected blame for the tuberculosis outbreak to both Baptiste and ISA 247, the investigational drug. This strategy fooled many people. The English media left them alone. Even Health Canada took the bait. But to buy into this line of thinking, one would have to twist the facts to fit the theory, a complicated process. Occam's razor tells us that the simplest explanation is the preferable one.

All previous ISA 247 clinical trials conducted by SFBC Anapharm had been reviewed and approved by our research ethics board, and they all included tests to rule out latent tuberculosis infection and tuberculosis disease. No one with either of these conditions would have been able to enter those clinical trials; they would have been denied due to a positive tuberculin skin test during the screening process. Each tuberculin skin test cost from twenty-five to forty dollars in 2005.

We know from the Evans Report that SFBC Anapharm did not administer any tests for tuberculosis when it screened potential research participants for this clinical trial. Instead, it relied on information volunteered by the potential participants about their travel history and whether they had latent tuberculosis infection. SFBC Anapharm shamelessly floated the irrational theory that Baptiste snuck his way into the clinical trial with latent tuberculosis infection by withholding information during the screening process. The company used phrases like "slipped through" and "deceived us" to describe Baptiste's alleged actions. It theorized further that once Baptiste was administered his first dose of ISA 247, his immune system was immediately suppressed, allowing his latent tuberculosis infection to come alive and become tuberculosis disease. As its theory goes, once Baptiste had tuberculosis disease, he infected the other research participants and study staff.

The problems with this theory are twofold. First, Baptiste was from Haiti. About 95 percent of Haitians are Black and they speak Haitian Creole, a language different from the French spoken by native Quebecers. SFBC Anapharm should have been able to deduce, from simply looking at and listening to Baptiste, that he might have been Haitian and thus might have had latent tuberculosis infection. To err on the safe side, SFBC Anapharm should have excluded Baptiste from participating in the study, not as a punishment, but to ensure the safety of the other research participants.

Second, as stated earlier, Mohsen noticed that Baptiste was not well on day 1 of the clinical trial, the day they were administered the first dose of ISA 247. As noted earlier, *Mycobacterium tuberculosis* is a slow-growing bacterium. A single day's exposure to ISA 247 was not sufficient for the drug to have any effect on Baptiste's immune system because the progression of latent tuberculosis infection to tuberculosis disease takes weeks or months.

The only explanation that fits the facts is that Baptiste had untreated tuberculosis disease when he entered the clinical trial. He passed the screening process because the screening process performed by SFBC Anapharm was inadequate. A thorough physical and proper history would have easily pointed to Baptiste's active illness, and a tuberculosis test would have confirmed these findings. The outbreak occurred because of the delay in isolating Baptiste from Mohsen, the other research participants, and the study staff. Those responsible for the tuberculosis outbreak were SFBC Anapharm and IRB Services. Isotechnika shoulders some of the blame because it failed to monitor how SFBC Anapharm was conducting the clinical trial.

SFBC Anapharm, by its own admission, believed that testing for tuberculosis hindered how quickly it could enrol research participants into its studies. It needed to find a research ethics board willing to approve ISA 247 studies without this important safety measure. IRB Services was the perfect partner in this forum-shopping scheme.

5

THE CONSEQUENCES OF NO CONSEQUENCES

THERE IS A KIND OF CONNECTIVE TISSUE THAT BINDS THE TRAGIC STORIES OF THIS book. It has sustained the memories of the unprotected and revealed the broken system of governance that yielded their harms. It has also provided us with the knowledge to create a brighter future.

The fact that tragedies keep happening is the first consequence of a system without checks and balances. When accountability is absent, researchers and research ethics boards believe that they are conducting themselves properly and make little or no effort to self-monitor. They are doomed to make the same mistakes over and over again.

BIORTHEX

You may recall from the book's introduction that Biorthex, a Quebec biotechnology company, terminated its study of a device for lumbar degenerative disc disease for financial reasons in April 2004, four months after it was initiated. At the time of study termination,

Biorthex's device had been implanted into the spines of eight research participants.

Biorthex had received authorization from Health Canada to conduct the study, which included a two-year follow-up period to monitor the safety of the implanted devices. When Biorthex refused to fund this follow-up period, we called Health Canada, expecting it to intervene, since Biorthex was clearly violating its own approved study protocol.

Health Canada bounced us around from office to office. We recounted our story to each person who took our call. Our telecommunications journey around Health Canada landed us in the office of the Health Products and Food Branch Inspectorate (which I'll refer to in short as the Inspectorate), where we were told that we would receive a callback.

As its name suggests, the Inspectorate conducts inspections to ensure the safety of Canada's health products and food. One of its duties is to assess whether and to what extent researchers are complying with the regulations as they conduct clinical trials. It has the authority to suspend a clinical trial until its inspectors are satisfied that researchers have corrected their research practices and have produced a plan to prevent their non-compliance from occurring in the future. It also has the authority to stop a clinical trial altogether for serious non-compliance.[1]

We never received a return call from the Inspectorate. Through its inaction, the government inadvertently immunized Biorthex from having to be accountable for its actions. We found ourselves alone in a fight for the rights of Biorthex's research participants that nearly ended up in a costly legal brawl.

ASCENTIA PHARMA

A few weeks later, we faced another study sponsor that was unhappy with a decision made by our research ethics board. One afternoon in May 2004, our board received 120 protocol deviations from one of our clients, Ascentia Pharma, a small Montreal-based company. Through these deviations, Ascentia Pharma was notifying us that it had failed to abide by the approved study protocol 120 times! The deviations ranged from innocuous procedural errors to major departures affecting research participants' rights, safety, and welfare, including the solicitation of informed consent. The research ethics board swiftly suspended the study until it could gather more information from Ascentia Pharma to determine its next course of action.

Instead of co-operating with our research ethics board, Ascentia Pharma sent a very loud and obnoxious lawyer to our offices to force us, under the threat of legal action, to lift the study suspension. While the lawyer's theatrics were entertaining, we held our position. We were obligated to notify Health Canada of the board's decision to suspend the study. We wrote directly to the Inspectorate explaining the rationale for the study suspension and requested its assistance with Ascentia Pharma's threats of legal action. The Inspectorate replied shortly thereafter, thanking us for bringing the matter to its attention but offering nothing in the way of support or relief.

Ascentia Pharma continued to refuse to co-operate with our research ethics board and instead decided to resort to forum shopping. It found a lenient alternative in IRB Services, which quickly resumed approval of the study as if the 120 protocol deviations hadn't even occurred. How Ascentia Pharma circumvented Health Canada's requirement that it disclose "the name, address and telephone number and, if applicable, the fax number and electronic mail address of any Research Ethics Board (REB) in Canada that has previously refused to approve the clinical trial protocol, its reasons for doing so, and the date on which the refusal was given"[2] remains a mystery to this day.

The Inspectorate missed a unique opportunity to address the insidious and harmful practice of forum shopping head-on. Without consequences, study sponsors like Ascentia Pharma will continue to deviate from their approved study protocols without understanding how this practice undermines the integrity of the study and the informed consent process.

Both Biorthex and Ascentia Pharma were running registration studies. This means that Health Canada reviewed their study documents, including their study protocols, and authorized the commencement of the studies by issuing letters of no objection. In both cases, the study sponsors failed to follow their approved study protocols. Our research ethics board had a duty to act on the sponsors' non-compliance. Health Canada had the same duty, yet, as we will see, it seems to pick and choose when to fulfill this obligation.

SFBC ANAPHARM

It was as if SFBC Anapharm had stolen a page from Ascentia Pharma's playbook. It also threatened our research ethics board with legal action after our board withdrew its ethics review services on September 23, 2005, following the contentious meeting described in chapter 2. SFBC Anapharm was also conducting registration studies, and as previously mentioned, we reached out to the Inspectorate for help in December 2005, directing a letter to Jean St-Pierre, the coordinator of good clinical practices within the Inspectorate, that outlined the profound issues we had encountered.

We purposely concealed SFBC Anapharm's name in our letter because of the legal threat disclosing it would pose. Jean St-Pierre formally responded to our letter on February 8, 2006. To each of our points he replied, "We invite and encourage you to provide us with specific details and examples of the issues so that we can take appropriate actions." The Inspectorate gave us no assurance that it would support us should SFBC Anapharm sue us for co-operating in an investigation.

The Inspectorate had nothing to lose. We were in a delicate situation: If we upheld our duty to co-operate with the investigation, we risked protracted and costly legal action from SFBC Anapharm, but if we didn't disclose the information, the Inspectorate might not investigate SFBC Anapharm and the test facility might never be held accountable for its conduct.

After much internal deliberation and weighing of consequences, we complied with Jean St-Pierre's request and co-operated with the Inspectorate concerning the allegations in our letter. After spending countless hours gathering the necessary documents for the Inspectorate and meeting with it on various occasions, we never heard from the Inspectorate or anyone at Health Canada again regarding SFBC Anapharm's conduct surrounding Henri's death or any of the other serious issues that we raised.

A TREASURE TROVE OF INFORMATION

Sometime in the early part of 2007, a banker's box arrived at our Montreal office containing a wealth of documents related to the tuberculosis outbreak and to Henri's death at SFBC Anapharm. As we sifted through the box's contents, it became clear that it contained a response from Health Canada to an Access to Information and Privacy request. The individual requesting the information wished to "obtain a copy of any reports, investigations, complaints, requested or received by Health Canada regarding individuals who underwent treatment by SFBC Anapharm in exchange for monetary contributions from January 1, 2005 to present [the date of the request]." It was not evident who requested the information or who sent us the banker's box.

The box contained a treasure trove of information regarding the inside workings of Health Canada and the Inspectorate with respect to these tragedies. The events that follow in this chapter were taken directly from the government's response to the request for information.

AN ASIDE ABOUT DAVID EVANS

David Evans, along with investigative journalists Michael Smith and Liz Willen, published a *Bloomberg News* article on November 2, 2005, called "Big Pharma's Shameful Secret." It was the culmination of their year-long investigation into the shocking and atrocious betrayals of research ethics at SFBC International's test facility in Miami, Florida. (As mentioned in chapter 2, SFBC International was the company that purchased Anapharm in 2002, creating SFBC Anapharm.) The article was replete with examples of breaches of informed consent practices; unethical confinement periods in overcrowded, filthy, and unsafe facilities; backloaded payment schemes; and coercive and threatening treatment of research participants, many of whom were undocumented immigrants. The article triggered a United States Senate investigation and the subsequent closure and ultimate demolition of the Miami test facility.

The article caught the attention of Mohsen, the research participant introduced in chapter 4, who had contracted latent tuberculosis infection while participating in a clinical trial at SFBC Anapharm's Montreal test facility in September 2005. When Evans learned of Mohsen's horrendous experience, he immediately set his sights on reporting the tuberculosis outbreak as a unique Canadian event linked to SFBC International's unethical practices south of the border. He worked quickly to gather the details of the tuberculosis outbreak so that the story could be published on the heels of "Big Pharma's Shameful Secret," while it was still fresh in people's minds.

THE TUBERCULOSIS OUTBREAK

On December 12, 2005, Evans requested a statement from Health Canada regarding the tuberculosis outbreak. He sought a quick turnaround from Health Canada, as his publishing deadline was rapidly approaching.

The next few days were sheer pandemonium at Health Canada. It was obvious that no one was aware that a tuberculosis outbreak had occurred at SFBC Anapharm four months earlier. The government staff were panic-stricken as they tripped over themselves trying to get in front of the tragedy before it was exposed by the media. The following excerpts from communications between the Inspectorate and other departments within Health Canada illustrate the chaos that ensued:

- December 12, 2005, 11:55 a.m. — "So far nobody seems to be aware of any reports of subjects having TB being enrolled in trials at Anapharm.... At this point we simply do not know if this comment from the journalist is valid."
- December 12, 2005, 1:33 p.m. — "I am working with the Inspectorate to validate if this case is true, but in the interim I also need to determine if any of us were notified about this."
- December 14, 2005, 10:16 a.m. — "Do we have a record of this trial? Did we issue a no objection letter? We need something definitive from HC [Health Canada] that we are aware of this trial.... We really need to find out what we know about this trial."
- December 14, 2005, 10:55 a.m. — "The story will criticize the company, but will also slam us if we can't demonstrate we're enforcing our regulations. We need to confirm to the reporter what we know and what we're doing about it. Deadline is today as the reporter is filing today."

The government's response was not surprising, since both Isotechnika (the study sponsor) and SFBC Anapharm had failed to properly report the serious adverse event and its tragic outcome to the authorities.

You may recall from chapter 4 that there was a discrepancy regarding the date when SFBC Anapharm first realized that Baptiste was suffering from tuberculosis disease. Isotechnika disclosed to Evans that SFBC Anapharm informed it of Baptiste's condition on September 3, 2005. But the information from the banker's box told a different story. It revealed an email dated September 19, 2005, from Isotechnika asking SFBC Anapharm to change the date it was informed of Baptiste's tuberculosis disease to September 15, 2005. Perhaps it did this to create the illusion that it was compliant with Health Canada's seven-day reporting requirement for serious adverse events, as it allegedly filed the event report on September 20, 2005.

To respect another Health Canada reporting requirement, SFBC Anapharm filed a single adverse event report fifteen days after the ISA 247 study ended, yet it failed to disclose that this single event caused an infectious disease outbreak that affected nine research participants and eleven staff members.

When Evans's story was published on December 15, Health Canada was spared the embarrassment of being totally unaware of the tuberculosis outbreak. One Health Canada employee wrote to her colleagues, "Department appears in a positive light…. It was not picked up by the newspapers in Canada." A big sigh of relief for a federal institution that boasts on its website that it "oversees clinical trials conducted by industry and academics to ensure the protection of participants and the integrity of the data."

With a potential media storm safely in the rear-view mirror, the Inspectorate went about its business of inspecting SFBC Anapharm and the ISA 247 study. The inspection was conducted on January 10, 11, and 12, 2006, with the objective of determining "whether the clinical trial was conducted in compliance with the approved protocol, Good Clinical Practices and the clinical trial regulations." On a personal note, I facepalmed when I read that the Inspectorate was interested in whether SFBC Anapharm complied with its study protocol, since neither the Inspectorate nor Health Canada had so much as flinched when we reported the protocol violations committed by Biorthex and Ascentia Pharma.

While it was important for the Inspectorate to determine whether the study protocol was followed, it should have first focused on whether the procedures within the study protocol conformed to current practices, guidelines, standards, and regulations. In doing so, it would have discovered that the SFBC Anapharm ISA 247 study protocol was missing an important screening test — namely, a test for tuberculosis.

Another historic tragedy, the TeGenero TGN1412 clinical trial, occurred in London, England, six months after the Montreal tuberculosis outbreak. The TeGenero TGN1412 case illustrates the importance of validating the appropriateness of study protocol procedures. In March 2006, eight men participated in this Phase 1 clinical trial conducted by a contract research company called Parexel on behalf of the drug company TeGenero. The study took place at Parexel's private research facility in London. It involved a novel monoclonal antibody designed to treat autoimmune and immunodeficiency diseases.

Minutes after the study drug was injected into the research participants, the six men who received the active component developed catastrophic, multi-organ failure, while those who received the placebo injection were not harmed. The injured men were immediately transferred to the intensive care unit of a nearby hospital. One research participant experienced severe swelling of the head, leading some to refer to this tragedy as the "elephant man" trial. Another spent four months in the hospital and had to have his toes and parts of his fingers amputated. All six men were told that they would likely develop autoimmune diseases or cancers as a result of their participation in the study.

Parexel, in defence of its conduct, which included the simultaneous injection of all research participants as opposed to the safer practice of sequential administration, quickly rebuked critics by stating that it had followed procedures. As our colleague Dr. Michael Goodyear wrote in the wake of this tragedy, "We have been assured repeatedly that proper procedures were followed, when the real question is whether they were the right procedures."[3]

In the case of SFBC Anapharm's ISA 247 clinical trial, it appears from the response to the information request that the Inspectorate did not consider assessing whether the study procedures were appropriate considering the potential for the study drug to harm research participants. Rather, the Inspectorate focused its assessment on determining whether SFBC Anapharm adhered to its standard general procedures for screening potential research participants, conducting a medical history and physical examination, administering the study drug, sampling blood, confining research participants, and reporting adverse events and serious adverse events.

Prior to the tuberculosis outbreak, our research ethics board had demanded that tuberculosis testing be used to exclude individuals with tuberculosis disease or latent tuberculosis infection. This condition had been placed on SFBC Anapharm's three previous ISA 247 studies that had been conducted under the auspices of our research ethics board. SFBC Anapharm knew this, and the Inspectorate did, too. However, this didn't stop the Inspectorate and SFBC Anapharm from working countless hours together to produce a guideline for clinical research studies involving immunosuppressive drugs.[4] They shamelessly presented it to the Canadian research enterprise as a brand new and significant revelation in clinical research. My colleague Martin Letendre referred to it as a public relations stunt.

The Inspectorate's report and findings were never disclosed to the public, and although the entire report was in the banker's box, every page of it was redacted. We will never know what the Inspectorate found at SFBC Anapharm or what the consequences of these findings were for the test facility or its research ethics board, IRB Services.

HENRI'S DEATH

Chapter 1 was dedicated to Henri's life and tragic death. When we received the banker's box of documents, it was terribly disheartening to learn that the Inspectorate did not launch an investigation into Henri's death after we disclosed it on December 20, 2005. Rather, its investigation was precipitated by a request made to Health Canada by an investigative journalist on February 9, 2006: "Please see if you can find anything about the death of a healthy subject at their [SFBC Anapharm's] Montreal clinic in September 2005."

It was clear from correspondence between various departments within Health Canada that the government was not aware of Henri's death. In what seemed like an effort to buy time, Health Canada wrote back to the journalist asking if they could be more specific with their request by disclosing who the study sponsor had been. The journalist replied with sharp sarcasm: "Wondering why Health Canada [is] unable to check on [the] death of a healthy person at a particular trial site in a particular month without being told the name of the sponsor? Are there so many healthy persons dying in trials there that more info is needed to isolate the one in question?" I'm sure I would have asked the same question.

Once again, Health Canada was caught flat-footed. On February 14, 2006, the Inspectorate contacted SFBC Anapharm's medical director, who confirmed that a death had occurred the previous September but said that, in his opinion, it was not related to the study drug. The medical director then demanded the name and contact information of the journalist. Health Canada's media relations department refused to release the journalist's identity to SFBC Anapharm.

Based only on data supplied to it by SFBC Anapharm, and without an inspection, the Inspectorate agreed with the medical director's assessment that Henri's death was not related to the study drug: "On reviewing the data we consider the cause of death unrelated to the medication tested (death occurring 10 days after a single dose of 50 mg)." In the same communication, the Inspectorate chastised SFBC Anapharm for not reporting Henri's death within the regulated time frame: "However, since it [Henri's death] happened within the sampling period and therefore within the time frame of the trial, it should have been reported to this agency in a timely manner." These communications were dated February 22, 2006.

On February 27 the Inspectorate requested a meeting with our research ethics board concerning Henri's death. During the meeting, we were undaunted in our disclosure of information. We took issue with SFBC Anapharm's recruitment campaign and how Henri's informed consent had been compromised as a result. We also bared our suspicions about Henri's health, given his age, and how he was deemed suitable for the clinical trial. We noted our concerns about the inspiratory rales heard during Henri's screening visit and the handwritten revisions to this finding that alleviated conditions that would have prevented Henri from participating in the study. The fact that these revisions were made on the same day that Henri was enrolled into the study did not escape us. We also emphatically expressed our doubts that Henri had shown no signs or symptoms of physical distress during his last visit to the test facility, less than one hour before he collapsed and subsequently died.

We argued against the medical director's assessment that Henri's death was not related to the study drug. We explained that up to twenty-five milligrams of bicalutamide would have been in Henri's body and that the test facility would have known exactly how much because it extracted a blood sample for the very purpose of measuring it two hours before Henri died. The drug concentration was vital to the determination of causality, yet it was never disclosed to our research ethics board or to Henri's family. Was the Inspectorate privy to this crucial piece of information, and if so, why did it keep it secret?

The Inspectorate finally conducted an inspection of SFBC Anapharm and the study on March 21, 22, and 23, 2006. Its report was included in the banker's box, but unlike the report on the tuberculosis outbreak, it was only partially redacted. Considering that the Inspectorate was investigating the death of a research participant, its findings seemed trivial, focusing on the test facility's paperwork handling. It was very troubling that, despite our assertions concerning the study drug, the report stressed that Henri's death was unrelated to it.

There were no data to support the medical director's rejection of the possibility that the study drug played a role in Henri's death. He had dismissively remarked that Henri probably died of old age, yet he took no responsibility for enroling the seventy-five-year-old into a clinical trial. One could surmise that his steadfastness was related to his loyalty to his employer, SFBC Anapharm, but we will never know.

WHERE ARE THEY NOW?

SFBC Anapharm never acted on its threat of legal action against our research ethics board. And it didn't seem fazed by the negative media reports and facility closures. Its unethical recruitment campaign continued for another ten years in Canada. Instead of changing its research practices, it simply changed its name.

Back in 2004, after acquiring Anapharm, SFBC had bought PharmaNet, a contract research company based in Princeton, New

Jersey. SFBC swallowed PharmaNet into its fold. The PharmaNet name was filed away until SFBC needed to reinvent itself after its troubles north and south of the 49th parallel.

In 2006, SFBC changed its name to PharmaNet and moved its main test facility from Miami to Toronto.[5] In the banker's box we found an email that had circulated within Health Canada. It was from its acting chief of media relations and stated, in part, "They [SFBC] were planning on expanding their facility in the states [United States] but then decided to expand in Cda [Canada] basically cause [because] regs [regulations] are looser." At least Health Canada wasn't shy about stating the quiet part out loud.

By early 2007, SFBC, with its shiny new PharmaNet name, was operating test facilities in Quebec City, Montreal, and Toronto. Despite everything we had disclosed to the Inspectorate, the red carpet was rolled out for SFBC to expand its operations in Canada to test its drugs on our population.

In 2011, PharmaNet was sold to inVentiv Health, which then merged with INC Research in 2018 to become Syneos Health, the name that it bears today.

As for IRB Services, it was never held accountable for forum selling, lenient reviews, or questionable research oversight practices, including the removal of tuberculosis testing in the ISA 247 study. In 2014, IRB Services was purchased by a research ethics board in the United States.

6

GAPS IN OVERSIGHT

TOO CLOSE FOR COMFORT

Some would say that the relationship between Health Canada and the pharmaceutical industry is a bit too close for comfort. That is certainly the sentiment of Dr. Joel Lexchin, a professor emeritus at York University and an emergency medicine doctor at University Health Network in Toronto. Dr. Lexchin has authored hundreds of peer-reviewed papers, and in many of these he has fearlessly voiced his concerns about Health Canada's relationship with the pharmaceutical industry.

In one paper, Dr. Lexchin noted that Health Canada routinely meets with pharmaceutical companies before and during their drug development to offer its advice on the types of clinical trials that would be required for it to approve a particular drug, and even on how to run the trials in the most cost-effective manner.[1] Dr. Lexchin worried that this activity — coupled with the fact that the majority of the operating costs of the Pharmaceutical Drugs Directorate, the body within Health Canada that approves drugs for sale — is funded by the pharmaceutical industry. He stated that this has the potential to compromise the objectivity of Health Canada's role in protecting public health. To illustrate his point, Dr. Lexchin introduced the following poignant analogy:

> Suppose a judge meets with the prosecutor before a trial starts, to discuss with the prosecutor how best to present her case. As the defendant, how confident would you be that the judge will be objective in coming to a decision?
>
> In the case of Health Canada and the pharmaceutical industry, the defendant is the Canadian public.

Like Dr. Lexchin, we were concerned that Health Canada had objectivity issues. A seventy-five-year-old man suitable for enrolment in a "healthy volunteer" study suddenly dropped dead. And for the first time in history, a tuberculosis outbreak occurred in a drug test facility. An objective oversight body would have sprung into action and properly investigated these tragedies.

What became of the Inspectorate's findings that SFBC Anapharm and its study sponsors failed to report the tuberculosis outbreak and Henri's death accurately and within the required reporting timelines? The Inspectorate was aware that SFBC Anapharm had data on the concentration of the study drug in Henri's system around the time of his death. Yet the response to the request for information that we received in the banker's box was silent on whether the Inspectorate demanded this vital information for its own causality assessment of Henri's death.

The public will never see the Inspectorate's full reports of its investigations of SFBC Anapharm, and no one will ever know if this test facility faced any repercussions for its actions. All we know is that SFBC Anapharm's business didn't skip a beat. It carried on conducting clinical trials as if these tragedies never occurred.

NARROW FOCUS

To understand the limitations of the Health Canada Inspectorate, we need to look at the legislation governing drugs, namely, the Food and Drugs Act. The act stipulates that before one conducts a clinical trial, authorization must be obtained from the regulator — that is, the Pharmaceutical Drugs Directorate of Health Canada, which regulates prescription pharmaceutical drugs. Before authorizing a drug for sale, it verifies that all of the safety, efficacy, and quality requirements of the Food and Drugs Act and its regulations have been satisfied.

Those regulations are Health Canada's Food and Drug Regulations. Part C, division 5 of the regulations outlines how one goes about obtaining regulatory authorization, and among other things, it places the responsibility on the clinical trial sponsor for ensuring that the clinical trial was approved by a research ethics board prior to initiation, that written informed consent was obtained from each individual before they participated in the clinical trial, and that the clinical trial was conducted in compliance with good clinical practices. The Inspectorate ensures that the clinical trials are conducted according to the regulations.

In 1997, I attended a meeting in Toronto sponsored by Health Canada where it presented a new guideline for clinical research published by the International Council for Harmonisation of Technical Requirements for Pharmaceuticals for Human Use. Founded in 1990, the council is a global initiative composed of regulatory bodies and the pharmaceutical industry and has evolved to include twenty-one member organizations and thirty-seven observers. The council creates guidelines for the development of drugs for their eventual registration and sale. On its website it describes its mission this way: "To achieve greater harmonisation worldwide to ensure that safe, effective, and high quality medicines are developed and registered in the most resource-efficient manner."

It developed a guideline so that council members could harmonize clinical trial conduct across global regulatory jurisdictions. Called the *ICH E6 Guideline for Good Clinical Practice* (which I will refer to as the Good Clinical Practice Guideline), it includes practice criteria for protocol development, informed consent, study monitoring, data management, and other important aspects of clinical trials. As a member of the council, Health Canada adopted this guideline and eventually incorporated it into its clinical trial inspection practices. As a consequence, all authorized clinical trials must comply with the Good Clinical Practice Guideline, and the Inspectorate's role is to monitor the compliance of regulated clinical trials to the guideline. That's it; that's all. The Inspectorate does not straddle the line regarding the ethical aspects of human research, except to verify that ethics review board approval and informed consent were obtained. If those boxes are ticked, it moves on. It doesn't concern itself with how the research ethics board reviewed a study or came to its decision or with how informed consent was solicited from research participants. These things are not in its wheelhouse.

AN ILLUSION OF PROTECTION

The party that funds a clinical trial, whether it be the government or a drug company, for example, is called the sponsor. The party that conducts a clinical trial is usually a licensed physician, and in the context of the regulations is referred to as the investigator. Unless one reads the Good Clinical Practice Guideline carefully, one might miss where it conflicts with the Health Canada regulations. Whereas the Health Canada regulations state that the clinical trial sponsor is responsible for obtaining informed consent, and obtaining approval from a research ethics board, the Good Clinical Practice Guideline shifts these responsibilities to the investigator leading the clinical trial.

In a 2007 paper, Martin Letendre and Sébastien Lanctôt pointed to the Canadian constitution as being responsible for the discrepancy between the Health Canada regulations and the Good Clinical Practice Guideline.[2] In fact, they noted that the federal and provincial governments are also at odds with each other. From a legal and constitutional standpoint, the conduct of health research by physician investigators falls under the jurisdiction of the provinces. At the federal level, Health Canada, having jurisdiction over the import and sale of drugs, relies on the clinical trial sponsor to ensure, through the sponsor's surveillance and monitoring, that the regulations are met. If the sponsor fails to conduct itself in accordance with the regulations, Health Canada has the authority to suspend its authorization to import or sell a drug for the conduct of the clinical trial. Letendre and Lanctôt concluded that this has created an illusion that the legal system of Canada protects research participants. Health Canada places the onus on clinical trial sponsors, whereas the provinces rely on the colleges of physicians and surgeons to oversee the conduct of clinical trial physician investigators. To this day, no provincial college has effectively assumed this oversight role.

In addition to the obvious conflict of responsibilities, neither the Health Canada regulations nor the Good Clinical Practice Guideline make any reference to how or based on what ethical standards one goes about soliciting consent from potential research participants. Nor do they address how or based on what ethical standards a research ethics board should review and approve human research. Nowhere was this more evident than in the Inspectorate's refusal to investigate some of the serious issues that we raised in our December 20, 2005, letter. For example, we contended that SFBC Anapharm was implementing an un-ethical recruitment campaign to attract research participants. The Inspectorate noted in its internal communications that "there is no specific restriction, from a regulatory point of view, to prevent a company from including incentives in recruitment advertisements for clinical trials" (English translation of the original French quotation). In an off-putting statement it even commended SFBC Anapharm for excluding the study sponsor's name and the name of the investigational product in its recruitment ads, as if this were some kind of extraordinary achievement.

Why couldn't the Inspectorate see that luring potential research participants with promises of large sums of money compromised the informed consent process? Why couldn't it see the harms eman-ating from forum shopping? Why did it gloss over our complaint about the involuntary confinement of a research participant? Why did it brush aside the fact that we were denied access to the test fa-cility to monitor a study? Why did it shrug off our concerns regard-ing Henri's death? The answer to all of these questions is simple: Violations of the ethical principles of human research are not in the Inspectorate's purview.

HEADING IN THE WRONG DIRECTION

Health Canada's Inspectorate began inspecting Canadian clin-ical trials in 2002 and disclosed the results of its inspections in multi-year reports. One such report, published on March 28, 2012, included aggregate data pertaining to inspections conducted and completed between April 2004 and March 2011.[3] Of the 329 clin-ical trials inspected in this seven-year period, the Inspectorate re-ported that it had assigned a non-compliance rating to 8 percent and rated 40 percent of its findings as major or critical.

Details of the Inspectorate's inspections have been made avail-able to the public since 2012 in a searchable database hosted on the Government of Canada website. The database includes information on the clinical trial sponsor, the drug under investigation, the clinical trial phase, the region of Canada where the inspection took place, the initiation date of the inspection, and the compliance rating. A hyperlink connects the compliance rating to details of the Inspectorate's findings. However, information that would identify the investigator or the investigative site under inspection is absent, making it very difficult for study sponsors to verify the competence of a particular investigator for future studies, or for research funding agencies to determine the eligibility of a grant applicant.[4]

Based on information in the Inspectorate's clinical trial database, 345 clinical trials were inspected in the next seven-year period. Of these, 12.46 percent were assigned a non-compliance rating, an astonishing 55.75 percent increase in non-compliance from the previous period. Very few clinical trials were inspected in 2020 and 2021 due to the pandemic, but by 2022, the number of inspections was almost 80 percent of the pre-pandemic volume. It should rattle the complacent to learn that 18.75 percent of the clinical trial inspections completed in 2022 were assigned a non-compliance rating.

These rates of non-compliance are heading in the wrong direction. If these data are new information to you, don't blame yourself. Health Canada has not made any attempt to ensure that Canadians are aware of this troubling trend. I would contend that the non-compliance numbers reported by the Inspectorate are probably on the low side. The Inspectorate doesn't consider any violations of research ethics principles in its inspections, nor does it include results from inspections by the United States Food and Drug Administration for studies co-registered south of the border. Investigative journalists from the *Toronto Star* have reported that Food and Drug Administration inspectors found "objectionable conditions" in more than 60 percent of the Canadian clinical trials they inspected.[5]

The Inspectorate's March 28, 2012, report began with its rationale for inspecting clinical trials: "Inspections of clinical trials are conducted to strengthen the protection of the rights and safety of clinical trial participants and validate the integrity of the data generated through the conduct of clinical trials." This is not entirely true. For the small percentage of clinical trials that it inspects each year, the Inspectorate only monitors compliance with the Good Clinical Practice Guideline. If informed consent was obtained and the clinical trial was approved by a research ethics board, the Inspectorate can check those boxes and move on. It does not assess how a researcher solicited informed consent or how a research ethics board reviewed the clinical trial.

Health Canada admitted as much in a September 2024 *Toronto Star* exposé entitled "Inside Canada's 'Exploitative' Clinical Trial Industry, Where Study Participants Say They're Incentivized to Lie — Even About Medications' Side Effects."[6] In the article, Health Canada stated that it does not oversee the informed consent process or the enrolment of research participants, including the ways in which they are remunerated or incentivized, because these elements "fall under the purview of REBs [research ethics boards]."

Twenty years have passed since Henri, Leticia, Baptiste, and Mohsen participated in their clinical trials. Yet, sadly, nothing has changed to protect research participants from the psychological harms brought about by excessive compensation schemes and long confinement periods. In fact, as revealed in the *Toronto Star* exposé, Canadian research ethics boards continue to approve clinical trials with precarious confinement periods and outrageous compensation schemes. They approve advertisement campaigns that lure potential research participants by glorifying the study's monetary compensation. The *Toronto Star* quotes a recent study advertisement aimed at post-menopausal and surgically sterile women: "Experience a summer as hot as your bank account! With compensations reaching heights of up to $17,150, imagine the endless possibilities for making this summer one to remember!"

Are these research ethics boards oblivious to how such compensation schemes potentially undermine a research participant's free and informed consent? I don't think so. A more logical rationale is that, in the absence of a system of objective oversight and accountability, research ethics boards, especially those in the private sector, are free to set their own approval standards, which may or may not protect research participants from such blatant undue influence.

7

THE ORIGINS OF RESEARCH PARTICIPANT PROTECTION

CLINICAL TRIALS, LIKE THOSE PRESENTED SO FAR IN THIS BOOK, REPRESENT ONE type of human health research. Some other types of human health research do not involve an intervention like a drug, and other types of research do not concern health at all. Although these types of research are conducted on humans, they do not fall under the scope of Health Canada's inspections.

In the *Toronto Star* exposé, Health Canada disclosed that "it uses a 'risk-based approach'" to determine which clinical trials to inspect, but it did not reveal how it defined risk or what percentage of registered clinical trials it intends to inspect on an annual basis. Its past goal was to inspect approximately 2 percent of registered clinical trials annually. Since the Health Canada Inspectorate does not oversee the informed consent process, the enrolment of research participants, or research participant compensation, it can be assumed that Health Canada's definition of risk does not include harms to a research participant's complete physical, mental, social, spiritual, and emotional health. How are the rights, safety, and welfare of research participants safeguarded? To answer this question, we need to journey back in time.

THE NUREMBERG CODE

Humans have been experimenting on other humans for centuries, most with the noble intention of contributing to the world's body of knowledge. Others have proceeded with reckless abandon, conducting unimaginable experiments on individuals who lacked the ability or opportunity to provide informed consent. Such were the experiments carried out by Nazi Germany during the Second World War.

Nazi physicians, mocking the Hippocratic oath they swore to uphold, committed the unspeakable upon humans they abhorred. The United States Holocaust Memorial Museum has grouped these experiments into three categories:[1]

- Survival of military personnel: These experiments were conducted by air force physicians to test the limits of altitude and temperature for the benefit of the military. In some experiments, prisoners were dropped from aircraft to determine the altitude at which they could land safely with a parachute. Other experiments involved freezing prisoners to test treatments for hypothermia.
- Drugs and other treatments: These experiments were conducted to develop treatments for injuries and illnesses encountered by the military. Physicians at concentration camps tested rudimentary vaccines and antibodies on the camps' prisoners, aimed at treating contagious diseases such as malaria, tuberculosis, and typhoid fever.

Other experiments included testing new drugs and surgical techniques and testing antidotes to phosgene and mustard gas exposure.

- Advancing racial and ideological goals: These unthinkable experiments were conducted to advance the racial and ideological goals of the Nazi world view. These included the experiments on twins by Josef Mengele (the "angel of death"), and experiments conducted to develop a procedure to mass sterilize and thereby eradicate those deemed genetically undesirable in the eyes of the Nazis.

The disturbing revelations about Nazi experiments led to the first ethical principles of human research.

On August 8, 1945, after the end of the Second World War, the Allied forces (the United States, the United Kingdom, France, and the Soviet Union) created the International Military Tribunal, composed of a judge and prosecution team from each Allied country. Its intention was to put the leaders of Nazi Germany on trial for war crimes, crimes against peace, crimes against humanity, and conspiracy to commit these crimes. The trials took place at the Palace of Justice in Nuremberg, Germany. Nuremberg was chosen by the Allies to symbolize the death of Nazi Germany, since Nuremberg had been a focal point of Nazi propaganda rallies leading up to the war. The trials became known as the Nuremberg Trials.[2]

The first trial included twenty-four of Nazi Germany's leaders, including Adolf Hitler, Joseph Goebbels, and Heinrich Himmler, even though they had all died by suicide either in the last days of the war or shortly before the trials began. Twelve trials followed the first trial, and one of these was called the Doctors' Trial.

The Doctors' Trial included twenty-three defendants, twenty of whom were medical doctors accused of conducting inhumane and

unethical experiments on concentration camp inmates. It concluded on August 20, 1947, with sixteen of the defendants being found
guilty. Jail sentences ranged from ten years to life imprisonment,
and seven defendants received death sentences. The tribunal's ju-
dicial verdict contained ten ethical principles for the conduct of
human research that became known as the Nuremberg Code.[3]

The first tenet of the Nuremberg Code states that humans must
provide their consent legally, voluntarily, freely, and with full knowledge of the experiments that they will participate in. In the words
of the code, "The voluntary consent of the human subject is absolutely essential. This means that the person involved should have
legal capacity to give consent; should be situated as to be able to exercise free power of choice, without the intervention of any element
of force, fraud, deceit, duress, over-reaching, or other ulterior form
of constraint or coercion; and should have sufficient knowledge and
comprehension of the elements of the subject matter involved as to
enable him to make an understanding and enlightened decision."
The other principles concerned the responsibilities of the researcher
to safeguard the individual's health, safety, and right to withdraw
from the research, and to ensure that the research is justified scientifically and will benefit society.

THE DECLARATION OF HELSINKI

The first general assembly of the World Medical Association took
place in Paris in 1947 and was attended by physicians from twenty-
seven countries, including Canada. According to the World Medical
Association's website, its mission was, and still is, "to serve humanity by endeavouring to achieve the highest international standards
in Medical Education, Medical Science, Medical Art and Medical
Ethics, and Health Care for all people in the world." It has created
global policy statements on a range of ethical issues related to medical
professionalism, patient care, research on humans, and public health.

In 1964, the World Medical Association published the *Declaration of Helsinki: Ethical Principles for Medical Research Involving Human Subjects.* It was developed from the Nuremberg Code's ethical principles, restating them to align with human research conducted by the medical community. Whereas the scope of the Nuremberg Code was broad and involved all human experimentation, the Declaration of Helsinki was more medically, or clinically, focused.

In addition to the Declaration of Helsinki, there are other related policies published and routinely updated: The Declaration of Geneva, first published in 1948 as a modern version of the Hippocratic oath; the Declaration of Tokyo, first published in 1975 as "guidelines for physicians concerning torture and other cruel, inhuman or degrading treatment or punishment in relation to detention and imprisonment"; and the Declaration of Taipei, first published in 2002. The Declaration of Taipei, a companion document to the Declaration of Helsinki, concerns the collection, storage, and use of identifiable data and biological material in human research.

The Declaration of Helsinki has had a major impact on clinical trials since its adoption. It has undergone numerous revisions since 1964, underscoring the progressive changes in medical and clinical human research and its ethical dimensions.

THE BELMONT REPORT

Revelations of abuse and exploitation of research participants continued in the era following the publication of the Nuremberg Code and the Declaration of Helsinki. The study that incited the publication of the Belmont Report was the Tuskegee Syphilis Study.[4]

The Tuskegee Syphilis Study was a horrific forty-year-long study conducted on Black men by the United States Public Health Service at the Tuskegee Institute (now Tuskegee University) in Macon County, Alabama. The study started in 1932 and its aim was to examine the natural progression of syphilis. It involved 399 Black men with syphilis and a control group of 201 uninfected Black men. The men agreed to participate in the study based on misinformation about its objectives and the promise of free treatments. None of the infected men received treatment for syphilis at any time during the study, despite the fact that penicillin was a known and effective treatment as early as 1940.

Four years into the study, it was clear that the infected men were developing complications of their disease at a higher rate than the men serving as controls, and the death rate of the infected men was almost twice as high as that of the control group at year 10. Yet the study continued.

In 1972, Jean Heller, an investigative reporter from the Associated Press, caught wind of the study, and her account of it was published in the *New York Times* and the *Washington Star*. Public outrage over the study exploded, leading the United States Senate to hold hearings into the study and to its immediate termination. Research participants who were still in the study at the time of its closure were immediately treated for syphilis and its related complications. In the ensuing years, the government extended treatment to the affected wives of the research participants and to their children who were born with syphilis.

In 1974, the United States National Research Act was introduced. It mandated the creation of regulations for the protection of human research participants and the formation of the National Commission for the Protection of Human Subjects of Biomedical and Behavioral Research. This commission recognized the ethical principles of the Nuremberg Code and the Declaration of Helsinki and set out to develop a workable set of general principles from them. These would be used to help researchers tackle complex ethical issues in human research that could not be resolved through the application of the previous codes. In 1979, the commission published its report, entitled *Ethical Principles and Guidelines for the Protection of Human Subjects of Research*.[5] It became more commonly known as the Belmont Report, named after the Smithsonian Institution's Belmont Conference Center, where the commission held most of its meetings.

The three fundamental ethical principles of the Belmont Report are respect for persons, beneficence, and justice. The methods used to recognize these principles are informed consent, an assessment of risks, and the appropriate selection of individuals for the research, respectively. Taken together, these principles provide a comprehensive foundation for ethical decision-making, leading to the resolution of ethical problems that arise when conducting research with humans.

CANADA'S TUSKEGEE

For a period of ten years beginning in 1942, close to one thousand starving Indigenous children were preyed upon by a government scientist.[6] This was Canada's Tuskegee.

At that time, the Nutrition Services Division of the Department of Pensions and National Health (now known as Health Canada) was led by a scientist by the name of Dr. Lionel Pett. Dr. Pett was lauded for introducing Canada's Official Food Rules, the precursor to Canada's Food Guide. He was consumed with scientific questions regarding the daily recommended intake of certain vitamins and minerals. But to answer these questions scientifically, he needed to conduct experiments on a population of malnourished individuals so he could systematically observe the effects of adding certain nutrients to their diets. It would be unethical, and unlawful, to impose a state of malnutrition on a healthy population, so his research interests were sidelined.

Between 1883 and 1997, in what has been called an act of cultural genocide, more than 150,000 Indigenous children were forcibly taken from their homes and placed in hundreds of federally run residential schools across Canada. It was widely known to the parents of these stolen children that they were starving in the residential schools. To verify the parents' complaints, the federal government sent investigators to the schools, and they quickly confirmed that the children were indeed suffering from severe malnutrition. The government tried to alleviate the problem by training residential school cooks to prepare more nutritious meals. It is not clear why these attempts failed.

When Dr. Pett heard about these Indigenous children, he jumped at the opportunity to conduct his long-awaited experiments on them. Why the Canadian government made the unfathomable decision to fund Dr. Pett's experiments is unknown. Some corporate sponsors, such as the Borden Company, a large North American food processor and manufacturer, contributed to the funding.

In one study, an experimental — and banned — fortified flour mixture was fed to some of the children. It contained bone meal, and children who were fed it were found to have increased incidences of anemia. In another study, children were denied dental care in order to observe the evolution of tooth decay and gingivitis. In all of the studies, the children were denied proper nutrition for the benefit of Dr. Pett and his research.

Dr. Pett's experiments breached the three fundamental ethical principles of the Belmont Report: respect for persons, beneficence, and justice. Respect for persons demands that individuals enter into research voluntarily and with adequate information. Notwithstanding the fact that children were involved and no added protections were provided, the experiments were conducted without the knowledge or consent of the children or their parents.

Beneficence demands that human research be justified in terms of the expected benefits versus the potential harms to research participants. This is normally accomplished through a risk assessment conducted by the researchers prior to starting the study. Dr. Pett conducted his unethical experiments with the knowledge that they would aggravate the harm the Indigenous children were already suffering. The experiments were not designed to address the children's nutritional states, and the children could not have derived any benefit from them.

The principle of justice demands that certain individuals or classes of individuals are not systematically selected for or excluded from research. It also demands that research excludes individuals unlikely to benefit from the research results. The Indigenous children were malnourished and vulnerable to manipulation, making them the perfect target for exploitation by Dr. Pett. They were not chosen because they would likely benefit from the research results. The purpose of the experiments was to understand the nutrients required in the diet of "Canadians." The experiments were not undertaken to solve the problem of malnutrition in Indigenous children held captive in residential schools.

The Truth and Reconciliation Commission's final report cites malnutrition as one of the main causes of death of children in residential schools.[7] Survivors were plagued with chronic effects of malnutrition, such as Type 2 diabetes, and research has indicated that it may have caused epigenetic changes that were passed on to the survivors' children and grandchildren.

CANADA'S GUIDELINE FOR ETHICAL HUMAN RESEARCH

The Nuremberg Code was well known after the Second World War, especially by the governments of the Allied countries, like the United States and Canada. Therefore, it's difficult to comprehend why the Tuskegee Syphilis Study and Dr. Pett's nutritional experiments continued, year after year, after the Nuremberg Code's publication. It is unimaginable that the governments of the United States and Canada were unaware of the unethical experiments they were funding.

The Nuremberg Code was fundamental to our current understanding of the ethical principles for all human research. The Declaration of Helsinki provided context to the Nuremberg Code for biomedical research and became a pivotal document over time. In 1978, one year before the publication of the Belmont Report, the Medical Research Council of Canada published the *Guidelines on Research Involving Human Subjects* (which I'll refer to as the Canadian Guideline). It provided researchers with practical information on the ethical conduct of human research, especially health research.

Both the Canadian Guideline and the Belmont Report required that potential research participants be treated as autonomous persons capable of choosing for themselves. The application of this principle involves a process in which potential research participants are provided with all of the information, in a comprehensible manner, necessary to make decisions about participating in research.

AN EARLY LESSON IN AGENCY

In 1984, I was studying toward a Ph.D. in molecular pharmacology in the Department of Medicine at the University of Alberta. I was fortunate to have Dr. Ken Wong as a supervisor. He was present and supportive, and he encouraged me — or simply didn't put obstacles in my way — when I would reach beyond my grasp. Dr. Wong was a biochemist and professor in the Faculty of Medicine. His office and lab were housed in the Division of Rheumatology, so my thesis topic, unsurprisingly, was suitably related. At that time, gold salts were administered to patients with arthritis, including rheumatoid and juvenile arthritis, to reduce inflammation. How gold salts achieved this was an enigma. My research explored this elusive action of gold salts in the inflammatory process using a type of white blood cell, the neutrophil, as my model.

Neutrophils are the first blood cells recruited to the site of infection or injury, and they are vital players in the orchestration of the body's local inflammatory response and healing process. Neutrophils roam through the bloodstream, and once they are activated by various inflammatory stimuli, they move in the direction of where they are needed. There they engulf and kill microorganisms and remove damaged tissue. By studying the molecular pathways of neutrophil stimulation and its responses, I was able to pinpoint the specific site of action of gold salts.

Neutrophils rapidly lose their responsiveness to stimuli once they are isolated from the blood. In fact, they become lazy and unpredictable within hours. So I had to run my experiments as soon as possible after I had isolated them from blood, which made for very long days in the lab. Medical students were a reliable source of blood for my research back then. On the days that I harvested neutrophils, I would linger outside the medical students' lecture hall forty-five minutes before classes started, in the hopes of finding someone willing to help. My department paid one dollar per tube of drawn blood, and since I always needed twenty tubes of blood, I was never hard-pressed to find an eager donor.

James was one such medical student. He stood well over six feet tall and weighed north of 250 pounds. I had never taken blood from James before, nor from anyone as big as James, but I was confident in my phlebotomy skills. I always took an awkwardly long time to find the perfect vein, but I was rewarded by never having bruised an arm. I was careful to lock eyes with James as I pushed the needle into his vein, and I engaged him in conversation as my hands busily exchanged blood-filled tubes with empty ones inside the syringe. About ten tubes in, James began to lose consciousness; the colour began to drain from his face, his eyes became heavy, and he slowly slid out of his chair onto the floor. As he drifted, I shamelessly steadied the syringe and kept the needle in his vein to get the remaining tubes of blood that I desperately needed for my day's experiments. James survived the blood draw unscathed. After eating a doughnut and drinking a glass of orange juice, he made it to his class on time, twenty dollars richer.

I've often reflected on my encounter with James. At that time, I understood that his role in my research was to supply me with blood. Until I stumbled upon the Canadian Guideline and the Belmont Report, it hadn't occurred to me that James, and all of the other medical students who contributed to my research, were *participants* in my research. Although James verbally consented to donate his blood for my studies, his consent was not informed. It was my responsibility to provide James with information concerning the risks of blood donation before he consented to participate in my research. The principle of respect for persons ensures that research participants like James have agency to make decisions about study participation.

TRI-COUNCIL POLICY STATEMENT: ETHICAL CONDUCT FOR RESEARCH INVOLVING HUMANS

In the late 1930s, at the bequest of the Canadian government, Dr. Frederick Banting, the Nobel Prize winner and co-discoverer of insulin, set out on a tour to visit medical researchers across the country, encouraging their pursuits and gathering information on their infrastructural needs. He found that there were few institutions outside the University of Toronto and McGill University that could support their researchers with the facilities, resources, and funding necessary to conduct their research.

With his data in hand, Dr. Banting presented his findings to the federal government and encouraged the creation of the Associate Committee on Medical Research. This committee resided within the National Research Council, and its initial mandate was to provide funding for medical research. These early efforts were quieted during the Second World War, as funds were diverted to the war effort. Tragically, Dr. Banting died in 1941 and the committee did not resume its activities again until the late 1950s. In 1960, Dr. Banting's vision of the establishment of the Medical Research Council of Canada was finally fulfilled. Its mandate was to advance biomedical research in Canada by supporting health research and the careers of established and young researchers and scientists.[8]

In 1992, the Medical Research Council merged with one of Canada's research funding agencies, the Canadian Institutes of Health Research. Six years later, in 1998, the Canadian Guideline was expanded to include all human research and was modernized and transformed into a policy called the *Tri-Council Policy Statement: Ethical Conduct for Research Involving Humans* (which I will refer to as the Policy Statement). The Policy Statement compiled the ethical guidelines supported by the three federal research funding agencies (the Canadian Institutes of Health Research, the Natural Sciences and Engineering Research Council of Canada, and the Social Sciences and Humanities Research Council of Canada) for the conduct of research on humans. All Canadian institutions that were eligible for funding from any of these agencies were required to follow the Policy Statement in the conduct and ethical review of their human research. A companion tutorial about the Policy Statement was created, and researchers were encouraged to complete it. The government left it up to each eligible institution to decide whether to make the tutorial mandatory.

Our research ethics board incorporated the ethical elements of the Policy Statement into its procedures, even though our board did not review publicly funded research until much later. At that time, the PDF of the Policy Statement that was available online from the government was extremely difficult to read. I recall that the font size was very small and the choice of font made the text look congested. So we requested permission from the Secretariat on Responsible Conduct of Research and from Public Works and Government Services Canada (now known as Public Services and

Procurement Canada) to republish the policy. By 2005, every client of our research ethics board, and many other community-based researchers in the private sector, had received a copy of the latest version of the Policy Statement, in both official languages and in a legible and inviting font, beautifully bound as a five-by-nine-inch hardcover book with a blue cover.

We followed up with our clients in the ensuing months to determine how the Policy Statement affected their research practices. We interviewed one particular client, an investigator in Quebec, about one year after he'd received the book. Although he recalled receiving the book and was grateful for it, he had no idea what the "TCPS" was. (The Policy Statement is commonly referred to as the TCPS.) In fact, he asked us if it was an infectious disease. As comical as his response was, it was a symptom of something more serious: Researchers, especially those in the private sector, did not feel duty-bound to read or observe the Policy Statement in the conduct of their research.

Unlike the Good Clinical Practice Guideline, which was fully incorporated into Health Canada's inspection program for drug research, the Policy Statement was not supported by any system of oversight. As policy-makers and funders of human research, the three federal research funding agencies had no way to ensure that the researchers they funded were conforming with the Policy Statement. As we'll see in the next chapter, relying solely on the good faith of researchers and research ethics boards to follow the Policy Statement and to conduct themselves in a manner that protects the rights, safety, and welfare of research participants can have dire consequences.

8

"CHANGE YOUR BRAIN WAVES; CHANGE YOUR LIFE!"

THE GATEWAY TO THE NORTH

Prince Albert is a small city in the heartland of Saskatchewan, on the south shore of the North Saskatchewan River. With prairie lying to its south and forest to its north, it has been appropriately named Saskatchewan's Gateway to the North, and the area's Cree name is Kistahpinanihk ("great meeting place"). For thousands of years the area, located in Treaty 6 territory, has been home to the Plains Cree, the Woodland Cree, the Swampy Cree, the Denē Peoples, and the Dakota and Métis Nations. According to Statistics Canada, Prince Albert's population was 37,756 in the 2021 census, with 16,120 (43 percent) identifying as Indigenous.

The Saskatchewan Rivers Public School Division operates thirty-two public schools in the Prince Albert area, twenty of which are elementary schools hosting children and adolescents from pre-kindergarten to grade 8. Riverside Public School is an elementary school within the division. The school implemented a curriculum to "decolonize the classroom" to ensure that its Indigenous students can grow and learn in a relatable environment, replacing many of its tools and resources with those that resonate with the children's lives, culture, and history.[1] However, by placing its trust in the competence of a popular researcher, and in a university research ethics board, this and other schools in the community inadvertently subjected their students to a study that was antithetical to this progressive curriculum.

AN UNLIKELY TRIO

Allan Markin was born in 1945 in Bowness, Alberta, a town that is now part of Calgary proper. He holds a bachelor of science degree from the University of Alberta and a few honorary degrees from other universities in Canada. Among his many awards, Allan Markin is an officer of the Order of Canada, a designation bestowed on him in 2008. He held various positions in the oil and gas industry before co-founding Canadian Natural Resources Ltd. in 1989, the largest independent producer of natural gas in western Canada and the largest producer of heavy crude oil in Canada. His success paved the way for him to become part owner of the Calgary Flames in 1994.

In 2012, at the age of sixty-six, he resigned as chairman of the board of Canadian Natural Resources and devoted his time to his new venture, Pure North S'Energy Foundation, a health and wellness initiative. Its core focus was to offer people alternative treatments for their medical problems. At some time in his own health journey, Allan Markin subjected himself to neurofeedback brain training at the Arizona-based Biocybernaut Institute, Inc.

The Biocybernaut Institute was founded by Dr. James Hardt, who describes himself on his website as a "true thought leader in the personal development field." Dr. Hardt holds an undergraduate degree in physics and master's and doctorate degrees in psychology, all from Carnegie Mellon University. The Biocybernaut Institute claims to use neurofeedback to train individuals to control their own brain waves so they can improve their lives. Dr. Hardt has been the president of the company since he founded it in 1983.

It should be noted that the Biocybernaut Institute's neurofeedback brain training is not accepted as a mainstream treatment among mental health specialists. In rigorous testing, neurofeedback has been shown to be no more effective than a placebo. A 2016 review of neurofeedback protocols states, "Although it is a non-invasive procedure, its validity has been questioned in terms of conclusive scientific evidence."[2] Yet the Biocybernaut Institute claims that its neurofeedback brain training has the ability to make people happy and smart, and Dr. Hardt has said that for some, it gives the ability to "levitate, walk on water and visit angels."[3]

Enter Dr. Carrie Bourassa. Dr. Bourassa professed to be Anishinaabe Métis. She claimed that she grew up in inner-city Regina in a family plagued by poverty, addiction, and violence, and that she faced racism on a daily basis. Dr. Bourassa alleged that despite the trials of her early life, with the encouragement of her Métis grandfather, she managed to break the cycle of intergenerational trauma. She excelled in school, earning three university degrees, including a doctorate in social studies from the University of Regina. She became a professor of Indigenous health studies at the First Nations University of Canada in Regina and a professor in the Department of Community Health and Epidemiology at the University of Saskatchewan. Dr. Bourassa was the chair of northern and Indigenous health at the Health Sciences North Research Institute in Sudbury, and in 2017 she was appointed scientific director of the Canadian Institutes of Health Research's Institute of Aboriginal Peoples' Health (now the Institute of Indigenous Peoples' Health), the third individual to ever hold this prestigious post.

Dr. Bourassa's world came crashing down in 2021, when it was revealed that her claims of Indigeneity were false. She had no Métis, First Nations, or Inuit heritage.[4] In fact, genealogical records revealed that she was descended from Swiss, Hungarian, Polish, and Czechoslovakian immigrants. Her parents were business owners, and she and her sister grew up in a middle-class neighbourhood in Regina's north end. Her father's 1982 Corvette was the envy of racing enthusiasts who frequented the local racetracks where he competed on weekends. Dr. Bourassa did not grow up poor or marginalized.

In her book *Truth Telling: Seven Conversations About Indigenous Life in Canada*, Michelle Good, author and lawyer of Cree ancestry, refers to people like Dr. Bourassa as "Pretendians." Good writes, "Pretendians only pop up where lucrative opportunities await them. We don't see them volunteering to share the profound hardship so many of us live with.... These fake Indians have neither the intergenerational knowledge that binds our people together as a community nor the intergenerational trauma, the scars of colonialism we uniquely bear, recognizable only to one another." Undoubtedly, Dr. Bourassa received educational funds and held positions that should have gone to Indigenous people who were genuinely eligible and deserving of them.

THE STUDY

In 2013, before she was outed, Dr. Bourassa was one of the prominent voices on Indigenous health matters in Canada. In hindsight, it was not surprising that she would align herself with Allan Markin and Dr. Hardt to develop a study aimed at improving the health of Indigenous children. The trio called their study the Prince Albert School Study, or PASS for short, and targeted Indigenous children from elementary schools in the Saskatchewan Rivers Public School Division.

The schools were chosen based on their high proportion of Indigenous students. Riverside Public School, Westview Public School, and King George Public School, all located within a six-kilometre radius, agreed to participate in the study on the condition that it obtain ethics approval from the appropriate research ethics board. As a professor at the First Nations University of Canada, Dr. Bourassa was required to submit the study to the University of Regina research ethics board for review.

THE FIRST STEP IN THE REVIEW

Because the University of Regina is a Canadian institution eligible for federal research funding, its research ethics board is obligated to adhere to the Policy Statement of the three federal research funding agencies. In fact, the university states on its website that research undertaken there conforms with the Policy Statement. The Policy Statement in effect at the time of the study submission was the 2008 version, published in December 2010. According to the Policy Statement, when the research ethics board received the study submission, the board was to conduct an assessment of risks in order to determine the level of review it required.

Risk is the potential for harm. Some risks are not as obvious as others, and some individuals are more sensitive to risk because of their life situations. With respect to human research, most of us think of risk in terms of physical harm, but there may also be risk of emotional, psychological, social, legal, or economic harms. Some risks are short-term, while others have the potential for lasting effects. Generally speaking, it is the duty of a research ethics board to consider the potential benefits of the study and weigh these against the potential for harm and the types of harms that may occur (the foreseeable risks). These are the components of a risk assessment. The three fundamental elements of the Belmont Report — respect for persons, beneficence, and justice — and the methods used to recognize them must be considered when a research ethics board conducts a risk assessment.

The risk assessment is required so that the research ethics board can apply the appropriate level of scrutiny to its review of the study. This is referred to as the "proportionate approach," and it must be applied to all reviews conducted by the research ethics board throughout the study's life cycle, including the initial review, continuing or annual reviews, ongoing reviews, and concluding review. In general, if research poses a minimal risk to research participants, its review can be conducted by less than a full board of members.

Research that involves children is justifiable only when the research question cannot be answered by a study involving adults. It is generally accepted that if the inclusion of children is justified, the risks to the children should be minimal. In some cases, however, the risks are above minimal. For such studies, the research ethics board must ensure that the study has the potential to benefit research participants directly and in equal proportion to the foreseeable risks, and that the relation of the potential benefit to the foreseeable risk is at least as favourable to research participants as other available alternatives would be.

As we will see in this chapter, the submission for the Prince Albert School Study lacked the basic information necessary for the University of Regina research ethics board to conduct a risk assessment. Risks were mentioned only once on the submission form, and even then only briefly: Referring to the probability that the study could cause emotional or psychological harm to research participants, the researchers stated, "There is a risk of anxiety or stress or discomfort." Yet the researchers gave no information to contextualize these potential harms or attribute them to a specific assessment or procedure. Nor, unsurprisingly, did they provide information to describe how they would mitigate and manage these risks.

The only acceptable decision options for the research ethics board were to defer the review of the study until appropriate and complete information was resubmitted or to disapprove it outright. Yet, somehow, the research ethics board accepted the submission for review and granted its approval.

A CASCADE OF BAD INFORMATION

To initiate a review by the research ethics board, the University of Regina required that researchers submit a twelve-page submission form along with various supporting documents. The study's submission form and supporting documents were outrageously deficient, and this should have sounded alarm bells for the research ethics board. It was missing important information concerning the study's objectives and methods, as well as information about the researchers involved and the roles they would play.

According to the submission form, the aims or objectives of the study were "to ultimately improve the school performances of the children and to improve the quality of their interpersonal relationships." A clear and logical rationale to support these objectives was absent from the submission, and no background information was provided that would have supported the rationale, had it existed.

Also missing was what should have been the submission's most pivotal document: the study protocol. It would have provided a rationale for the study and described results from previous studies to support the study's objectives. With this information, the research ethics board would have been able to evaluate the appropriateness of the type of study proposed and the justification of why it was chosen. This is important to ensure that the stated study type is the one best suited to address the study's objectives, compared to other study types.

The study submission indicated that the researchers would be implementing a "mixed methods" methodology in the study, meaning that they planned to collect, analyze, and interpret both quantitative (numerical) and qualitative (non-numerical) data. No justification was provided for choosing this study type, nor did the researchers indicate if other types were considered.

Intrinsic to the evaluation of ethical acceptability by a research ethics board is a review of the study's methods. What follows are some of the methods presented in the study submission and those that were blatantly absent. Even those presented were scantily described, which should have made it impossible for the research ethics board to evaluate them.

The study design describes the approach the researcher will take to address the stated study aims or objectives. Despite this study's lack of clear objectives, a study design was presented that included three equal treatment arms: (i) nutrition and vitamins plus neurofeedback brain training, (ii) nutrition and vitamins alone, and (iii) neurofeedback brain training alone. Nine months into the study, the research ethics board approved an amendment to the study that eliminated the third treatment arm. No rationale for this major study design change was provided.

Further, virtually no information was provided to describe how research participants would be allocated or randomized to the treatment arms. This would have made it impossible for the research ethics board to evaluate how treatment assignments would be controlled for subjectivity and bias.

No descriptions of Pure North S'Energy Foundation's nutrition and vitamins or the Biocybernaut Institute's neurofeedback brain training were provided on the submission form or in any of the appendices that accompanied it. The administration frequencies of these treatments were also missing. This raises the question of whether these proposed interventions should have undergone prior review by Health Canada to ensure they were safe and justified for use in a research study.

The submission stated that original data obtained from the study, including the questionnaire data, would be collected by researchers from the First Nations University of Canada and that full access to the data would be granted to researchers from the Biocybernaut Institute and the University of Calgary. The submission also indicated that Pure North S'Energy Foundation would be collecting data associated with blood and urine samples, yet the significance, number, and types of tests, and details of the analyses were not disclosed. No details were provided regarding how data access would be monitored and secured, how the data would be analyzed, and to whom the results would be reported.

Adolescent children aged twelve to fifteen years were to be recruited for the study directly from elementary schools in the Saskatchewan Rivers Public School Division. According to the submission form, three elementary schools were targeted in the division because they had a high proportion of Indigenous students. The schools, with the percentage of Indigenous students stated in the submission, were Riverside Public School (87 percent), Westview Public School (70 percent), and King George Public School (no percentage provided). Seven months into the study, it was amended to include W.J. Berezowsky Public School.

The submission indicated that teachers and staff from the participating elementary schools were responsible for recruiting students for the study. The schools were to distribute a trifold study pamphlet to their students, and those wishing to participate were encouraged by their teachers to apply online along with one parent or legal guardian. Given the power imbalance between the staff and the adolescent students, the research ethics board should have requested more details regarding the recruitment process in order to assess how the researchers would prevent and mitigate undue influence by the individuals in authority.

The recruitment pamphlet was submitted to the research ethics board. On the cover page, the title "Prince Albert School Study" appeared atop an image of a bison in front of the foothills. On the bottom of the pamphlet was the phrase "Change your brain waves; change your life," which added to the potential for undue influence on the adolescent students and their parents. Written in the style of a sales pitch, the pamphlet was short on specifics of what Pure North S'Energy Foundation's nutrition and vitamins and the Biocybernaut Institute's neurofeedback brain training entailed.

The pamphlet requested that individuals interested in participating in the study (both adolescent students and their parents or legal guardians) apply via email. They were asked to include their full names, dates of birth, phone numbers, email addresses, home addresses, and answers to the following:

- which treatment group they wished to participate in (Pure North S'Energy Foundation's nutrition and vitamins or the Biocybernaut Institute's neurofeedback brain training),
- why they wanted to participate in the study,
- what they hoped to get out of the program, and
- what "commitment" meant to them.

The email was to be directed to an address at the Biocybernaut Institute, yet nowhere in the pamphlet was there any mention of the measures that would be taken to protect their personal information or who would contact them to confirm their participation.

The process of soliciting an individual's consent must minimize the possibility of excessive motivating factors or undue influence in decision-making and allow ample time for the individual to discuss the study, seek advice, and ask questions. In the research ethics board submission, the pamphlet was attached to the four-page informed consent form as an appendix. Nowhere on the submission form was the process for soliciting consent from potential research participants described. By consenting to participate in the study, individuals were confirming that they read and understood the contents of the pamphlet. Therefore, the pamphlet formed an integral part of the informed consent form.

The pamphlet dedicated space to Pure North S'Energy Foundation and boasted unsupported claims that its services and products made people "feel better and live longer." Similarly, the pamphlet brazenly hailed the applications and features of the Biocybernaut Institute's neurofeedback brain training without providing any evidence to support them. These features included a greater than 50 percent increase in creativity; a greater than 11.7-point increase in IQ; reversal of brain aging; more happiness and joy; less fear and anxiety; more patience and understanding; peak performance in sports, intellect, and relationships; and beneficial long-term personality changes.

Absent from both the pamphlet and the informed consent form were details of Pure North S'Energy Foundation's treatment intervention, including the specific types of nutrients and vitamins and their concentrations, doses, and modes of administration. The risks associated with taking these nutrients and vitamins were also missing. No information or details concerning the Biocybernaut Institute's neurofeedback brain training intervention were provided either.

Both the informed consent form and the pamphlet disclosed that research participants would be able to select their preferred study treatment, with their options stated as the Pure North S'Energy Foundation's nutrition and vitamins or the Biocybernaut Institute's neurofeedback brain training. Yet the third treatment arm of the study included both treatments and it was not clear how research participants would be allocated to that arm.

The documents stated that those choosing to participate in the Biocybernaut Institute's neurofeedback brain training would be escorted from Prince Albert to Saskatoon and then flown to Victoria, British Columbia, where they would be housed at a bed and breakfast, with all of their meals and expenses paid for over the seven days of the study and the travel days. Those who did not choose the Victoria excursion would receive Pure North S'Energy Foundation's nutrition and vitamins at home in Prince Albert. The imbalance between the options constituted an excessive motivating factor for potential research participants that should have concerned the research ethics board members.

The informed consent form did not mention that research participants would be required to submit to blood and urine testing or at what frequency this testing would occur. Also missing was disclosure of the risks associated with blood testing. The pamphlet touched on the subject this way: "When enrolled in the Pure North S'Energy wellness program the participants will have a complete health assessment (including blood and urine analysis) to determine your current nutrition and health levels." This implicit disclosure should not have been acceptable to the research ethics board.

Every research participant has the right to withdraw their consent to participate in a research study at any time and for any reason. The research ethics board must assess the impact of this withdrawal on the research participant, the research, and the research data. Provisions for withdrawal were present in the study's informed consent form; however, to withdraw from the study, the participant needed to formally convey their request, either in writing or orally to the study staff. This type of condition is unethical because it can create a barrier to or suppress a research participant's right to withdraw their consent at any time and for any reason. Furthermore, no information was provided in the submission to explain how research participants at the

Biocybernaut Institute's facility in Victoria would be returned to Prince Albert if they withdrew their consent to participate while at that facility.

The principal investigator or researcher of the study was listed as Dr. Carrie Bourassa, with co-principal investigators Dr. James Hardt of the Biocybernaut Institute, Dr. William Pelech of the University of Calgary, and Dr. Betty Bastian, also of the University of Calgary. No supporting information regarding the investigators' qualifications and credentials, such as curricula vitae, accompanied the submission, and the roles of the investigators in the study were not disclosed. Apart from their designations as co-investigators, neither Dr. Pelech nor Dr. Bastian were mentioned again in the submission. It was not clear what role the University of Calgary was to play in the study.

The research ethics board should have ensured that the study's investigators were qualified to conduct the study based on their relevant credentials, education, training, and experience. Without any supporting information, the research ethics board would not have been able to make any determinations about the investigators' suitability for the study, including their familiarity with the methodology and their ability to work with the proposed study population. It follows, then, that in the absence of information on the investigators' affiliations and roles in the study, the research ethics board had no way to assess if they had any real, potential, or perceived conflicts of interest that could impact the study.

The submission listed the funding source for the study as "internal," indicating that the First Nations University of Canada or another affiliated university was funding it. However, the submission also confirmed that Pure North S'Energy Foundation was a major funder of the study and would supply the majority of the funds needed to undertake it.

Pure North S'Energy Foundation was more than a mere research funder. The submission stated that staff from Pure North S'Energy Foundation would be intimately involved in the enrolment of research participants, the administration of nutrition and vitamins, blood and urine sampling, and the collection and storage of study data. However, no one from Pure North S'Energy Foundation was listed as a study investigator or co-investigator. This omission should have prompted questions from the research ethics board regarding conflicts of interest, since the main commercial interest of Pure North S'Energy Foundation was its nutritional supplements and vitamins.

PASS GOT A PASS!

The Prince Albert School Study (PASS) submission was received by the University of Regina research ethics board on August 20, 2013. Despite the submission's abundance of serious flaws, the research ethics board approved the study on November 12, 2013. Soon after the submission was received, the administrator and chair of the research ethics board deemed that it posed more than minimal risk and forwarded it for review to the full board of seven members, none of whom had the relevant expertise or sufficient experience to properly assess it. The members commented that the study "seemed somewhat out of the normal range of research that we consider," yet they did not seek outside expertise to aid in the review.

Some members expressed skepticism about the study, but in the end, they were satisfied that it "seem[ed] to cover all of the required elements" and approved it. There is no reasonable explanation to account for the research ethics board's decision to allow the study to proceed.

As mentioned earlier, the study was amended at least twice in the year after its approval, giving the research ethics board pause to revisit and reflect on its decision. Some of the amendments, such as eliminating one of the three treatment arms and increasing the sample size, represented major changes to the study's design. It was incumbent on the research ethics board to ensure that these changes did not negatively impact the integrity of the study or the rights, safety, and welfare of the research participants. For example, it is unethical to conduct a study if the sample size (number of research participants) is too small to answer the research question. It is also unethical if the sample size is too large. Both situations place research participants at risk unnecessarily and waste resources. The original study submission did not describe how the researchers estimated the sample size for the study. Therefore, the research ethics board had no way of assessing amendments that altered the sample size or design of the study.

As you may recall, Dr. Bourassa was a professor at the First Nations University of Canada at the time the University of Regina research ethics board received the study submission. She implicated both the First Nations University of Canada and the Saskatchewan Rivers Public School Division in the study without their authorization. The logo of the First Nations University of Canada appeared in the top left corner of the informed consent form, and a section of the pamphlet included this short description of the university: "FNUniv is a unique Canadian institution that specializes in Indigenous knowledge, providing post-secondary education for Aboriginal and non-Aboriginal students alike within a culturally supportive environment. First Nations University will provide research expertise to the study. Questionnaires and interviews will be processed in the FNUniv laboratories." In November 2014, senior officials at the First Nations University directed Dr. Bourassa to remove the institution's name from any association with the study, as it had not been aware that the study had been submitted to the University of Regina research ethics board on its behalf.

The study was initiated at four elementary schools in the Saskatchewan Rivers Public School Division without having been approved by the division's board of directors. On November 21, 2014, upon realizing that the study was taking place, the Saskatchewan deputy minister of education instructed the school division to withdraw its involvement in the study. There is no record that the research ethics board ever received study amendments removing the study's affiliation with the First Nations University of Canada or the participation of the Saskatchewan Rivers Public School Division.

What Dr. Bourassa did next should have caused the research ethics board to suspend the study. On December 1, 2014, Dr. Bourassa filed a study closure form with the University of Regina research ethics board. In it she resigned from the study. She stated, "In consulting with my senior management I feel that I have too many projects and this particular project is not the best fit for me at the present time." At the time of her resignation, sixty research participants had been enrolled in the study, and Dr. Bourassa recommended that the study continue under the supervision of Dr. Pelech from the University of Calgary and other "senior scholars" in Saskatchewan. One section of the study closure form posed considerable concern. To the question "Since receiving the original ethics approval, have any ethical concerns arisen?" Dr. Bourassa answered yes. Her accompanying comments were redacted by the University of Regina in its response to an Access to Information and Privacy request.

The University of Regina research ethics board did not suspend the study. Instead, it allowed the study to continue until early 2016 under the supervision of a new principal investigator, Dr. Jo-Ann Episkenew, the director of the University of Regina's Indigenous Peoples' Health Research Centre.

HARMS WERE INEVITABLE

The study was exposed in a series of articles and news reports by Geoff Leo, a senior investigative journalist from CBC

Saskatchewan.[5] Leo and his CBC colleagues visited Dr. Hardt at his facility in Sedona, Arizona, and interviewed study staff and research participants from the Prince Albert School Study as part of their investigative work.

Dr. Hardt and the Biocybernaut Institute claimed that their neurofeedback brain training relieved stress, anxiety, and other symptoms of post-traumatic stress disorder and that they did this at a faster rate than traditional treatments and therapies. To make such claims, Dr. Hardt and his colleagues would have needed indisputable data from properly designed studies with affected adults. There is no evidence that such studies were ever conducted, nor are data publicly available to prove that such studies existed. This means that the claims were simply theories based on anecdotal data at best. There is no doubt that Dr. Hardt was conducting exploratory research on the students of Prince Albert. In reference to the children, he told CBC, "We have a novel group, we have a powerful technology. Let's see what happens."[6]

Dr. Hardt's view of Indigenous people formed the basis for conducting the Prince Albert School Study. He referred to the Indigenous people as having "more profound post-traumatic stress disorder than returning war veterans." As for targeting adolescent children from Prince Albert, Leo quoted a piece Dr. Hardt wrote for a journal in 2013: "The schools up there have up to 85 per cent Aboriginal students and many teachers are Aboriginal so it would be a really good case study; a lot of drugs, a lot of absenteeism."[7] This overt stigmatization was on full display in the study with the inclusion of one questionnaire, aimed at post-deployment veterans, that asked about post-traumatic stress disorder and another that focused on substance abuse and addiction.

As I mentioned earlier in this chapter, harms from research can take many forms, and researchers must anticipate such harms so that they can be properly analyzed. To address how the researchers could have prevented or mitigated these harms, it is important to analyze what contributed to them.

One possible contributing factor that led to the study's psychological harms was the overt undue influence exerted on the research participants by teachers and school staff. In human research, undue influence can be described as the use of persuasion through authority figures or the offer of an excessive or inappropriate reward in order to obtain research participation or compliance. Teachers and school staff played an important role in the recruitment for and management of the study. To prevent undue influence, study recruitment and management should have been implemented by individuals who did not have a prior relationship, especially a power relationship, with the research participants.

Aryn Peterson, a social worker with the Saskatchewan Rivers Public School Division, was one such authority figure associated with the study. She actively communicated with research participants through her public Facebook page. Below are some of her Facebook posts:

- Hi Prince Albert School Peeps!... Private message me if you wanna go to British Columbia! It's way nicer there than here right now!!!!!
- For those of you on the Vitamin Program ... The Vitamins we are all taking are valued at $3000 a year which is amazing that we get them for free! People have shared that they feel 100% better when taking their Vitamins and have more energy, lost weight and have reduced any medications.
- For anyone who can recruit us some new families ... will receive a $20 Walmart gift card! I need you to recruit them and bring them on either

Oct 13 or 14th to the pizza party and they need to stick in the program for over 6 months.
- We will be having a Pizza Party at Vincent Massey on Thursday at 5 pm. For those of you needing your paperwork done please stop by. We also need new families so send some new recruits our way!... [I]f you come do your paperwork we will give you $25 — I also can hand out all your t-shirts if you want stop by!

The power imbalance between Aryn Peterson on the one hand and the students and their parents or legal guardians on the other created a setting for undue influence. Offering students a monetary reward to recruit their friends into the study was inappropriate and a blatant example of undue influence. This reward or finder's fee is not ethically acceptable in human research because it can increase the likelihood that the person doing the referring is motivated by the promise of a reward and is not acting in the best interest of the individual they are referring.

Aryn Peterson disclosed various unsupported and exaggerated benefits of the study (feeling better, losing weight, taking fewer medications), and in doing so violated the first ethical principle of the Belmont Report: respect for persons. By presenting non-factual information as facts, Aryn Peterson deprived research participants of their ability to exercise free will in their decision-making.

The details of the Biocybernaut Institute's neurofeedback brain training were not disclosed to the research participants before their Victoria sojourn. From CBC's reporting we learned that the research participants became aware of what the brain training entailed only after they arrived at the facility. The procedure involved pasting electroencephalogram electrodes to the participant's scalp and then having them sit in a dark chamber. Study technicians monitored the participant's brain activity in a nearby room and converted the brain waves to sound cues. These sound cues were then fed to the research participant while they sat alone for hours listening to them in the dark chamber. An elderly woman participating at the Victoria facility as her grandchild's guardian suffered a panic attack brought about by claustrophobia in the dark chamber. No medical staff were present to attend to her.

A twelve-year-old research participant, obviously disturbed by the procedure, described the sound cues as "scary trumpets." On the third day of the experiment, feeling betrayed, this participant and her mother requested to withdraw from the study and return to Prince Albert. Although they had been told that they had the right to withdraw, it was an impossibility once they were in Victoria. As with almost all of the research participants, they did not have the financial means to get back home on their own. Trapped at the facility, they completed the brain training, feeling like they had no other choice. Other research participants shared similar stories with CBC.

Not disclosing study details undermines the ethical principle of respect for persons by masking or outright hiding information an individual needs to make a free and informed decision regarding participation. The truth concerning the study details became clear only once they began participating in the study, when they faced the horror of what they had agreed to endure.

In addition to the daily episodes in the dark chamber, research participants were subjected to intense discussions aimed at reliving their most traumatic moments, often in front of other participants and study staff. After returning home from Victoria, some participants interviewed by CBC disclosed that they experienced anxiety, depression, and feelings of being disconnected, and one research participant reported feeling suicidal. These are all common emotional reactions to trauma and to a retraumatizing event. No efforts were made by the study staff to prevent or mitigate these psychological harms or to treat the affected research participants.

The research participants, especially the adolescent children, also experienced social harms. Breaches of privacy can be forms of social, legal, or economic harms. In children between the ages of twelve and fifteen, the harm is primarily social. Privacy is the right and control that individuals have over sharing themselves with others and includes their thoughts, identity, and information contained in their biological materials. Confidentiality is the protection of a person's private information. People who disclose their private information in a relationship of trust have the expectation that it will not be shared with others without their permission. This was the expectation of the research participants enrolled in the study.

For a period of approximately twelve months during the study, Aryn Peterson routinely posted communications to the students on her public Facebook account, either tagging them or calling them out by using their first and last names in her posts. More than once, she invited current and potential students to pizza parties where the personal nature of their study participation would be exposed. These individuals had an expectation of privacy as they contemplated study participation, while they were enrolled in the study, and after the study was completed. To breach their privacy violated the ethical principles of respect for persons and beneficence.

Aryn Peterson closed her Facebook account shortly after Geoff Leo exposed the Prince Albert School Study in the news media. In screenshots that I had captured of her posts, I counted over fifty names of students and their parents or legal guardians who were already enrolled in the study or were potential research participants. All of these individuals had an expectation that Aryn Peterson, and all of the study staff, would safeguard their private information.

WHERE WAS THE OVERSIGHT?

What is the primary role of a research ethics board? Although the duties of research ethics boards vary among Canadian institutions, they would all agree that their primary role is to safeguard the rights, safety, and welfare of research participants and potential research participants through their review of planned and ongoing human research. Research ethics boards have the right to monitor the informed consent process and other research procedures to ensure that the researchers are not deviating from the approved research. However, this right is seldom exercised.

How well a research ethics board performs its role and upholds its duties is anyone's guess. Errors made by research ethics boards may be realized only after research participants experience harm. Such was the case with the Prince Albert School Study. As arbiters of whether a research study can proceed or not, research ethics boards cannot afford to err, because each mistake has the potential to directly or indirectly affect human lives.

What should the acceptable error rate be for a research ethics board? Five errors per study? Three? If your child or parent was a research participant, what error rate would be acceptable to you? For me, the answer is clear: zero. Zero tolerance is achievable only through good and ethical governance, of which oversight and accountability are intrinsic components.

9

GOOD AND ETHICAL GOVERNANCE, PART I

GOVERNANCE REFERS TO THE STRUCTURES AND PROCESSES THAT ORGANIZATIONS and societies implement when making decisions and exercising authority. Experts make an important distinction between *good* governance and *ethical* governance — and both are required.

Good governance emphasizes the principles of transparency, accountability, responsiveness, equality, and inclusiveness in the decision-making process. It follows the rule of law and is participatory and consensus-oriented. Good governance promotes efficiency and effectiveness and the well-being of all stakeholders, and it fosters a just and inclusive environment. *Ethical* governance ensures that decision-making is not only good (inclusive, legal, efficient, and so on), but that it is guided by moral values and principles such as honesty, integrity, fairness, and respect for human rights. When applied to human research, good governance and ethical governance mandate that systems of oversight and accountability exist and are implemented to ensure that the research complies with the laws and regulations, and that the ethical principles of human research are respected throughout its life cycle.

One of Canada's experts in human research governance is our colleague Dr. Michael McDonald. Over his successful career, Dr. McDonald has researched areas of theoretical and applied ethics, including issues related to evidence-based protection of research participants and the proper governance of human research. According to Dr. McDonald and his colleagues, the governance of human research must promote socially beneficial research, ensure that the rights and welfare of research participants are protected uniformly, and build trust between the research community and society: "We need both socially beneficial research and the protection of human subjects. Without these two together, there is the serious risk of undermining the fundamental trust relations that underwrite health research — the public's trust in researchers, research institutions and sponsors and more specifically the trust of research subjects whose continuing participation in research is so essential not only to health research but also to health care. Governance is about maintaining, enhancing and, where necessary, restoring trust in transparent, accountable and effective ways."[1] These objectives cannot be met without systems of oversight, or what Dr. McDonald refers to as "virtuous learning loops" involving auditing (quality assurance), inspections, and quality improvement.

Dozens of errors were made by the University of Regina research ethics board in its review of the Prince Albert School Study. In his exposé, Geoff Leo reported that the University of Regina's vice-president of research, Dr. Christopher Yost, blamed the errors on the poor policies and practices of the research ethics board at that time.[2] Dr. Yost added that, had the study been submitted to the research ethics board today, the review process would be more robust. Dr. Yost did not support his assertion with any evidence. It should be noted that, in the decade that has passed since the approval of the Prince Albert School Study by the University of Regina research ethics board, no new governing documents have emerged that would have triggered the change to the board's policies and practices that Dr. Yost claimed.

The University of Regina is an eligible institution in the eyes of Canada's research funding agencies, meaning that its researchers are entitled to apply for federal research funds. To receive such funds, the university has agreed to abide by the policies of the federal research funding agencies, including the Policy Statement. Breaches of the agencies' policies can be reported to the Secretariat on Responsible Conduct of Research (which I will refer to as the Secretariat), which has the authority to investigate the breaches and recommend appropriate consequences to the panels and agencies if required.

The University of Regina, through its research ethics board, committed numerous breaches of the Policy Statement in its review of the Prince Albert School Study. A group of us reported these breaches to the Secretariat for investigation, which prompted a meeting between the Secretariat and Dr. Yost. The results of that meeting were conveyed to us by Dr. Yost in an email. He wrote, in part, "We have contacted and met with the Secretariat regarding your correspondence and confirmed that this matter is not in their remit given the funding source for the study."

Whoa! This was new information for the research community. The Secretariat's executive director subsequently confirmed to Geoff Leo that the Secretariat has the authority to investigate breaches of its policies only if the research is funded by one of the three federal research funding agencies. In her interview with Leo, the executive director stated, "In the case of the Prince Albert School Study, this research was not funded by the federal research granting agencies and so it is outside of the Secretariat's jurisdiction."[3]

Leo refuted this by quoting the government's research ethics website, which states that the policies of the federal research funding agencies apply "to agency and non-agency funded research."[4] The executive director "replied that the government hopes research institutions will follow the policy when it comes to privately funded studies, but its enforcement powers only apply to government-funded research."[5] Hoping that research institutions will comply with the policies is not good governance.

The executive director continued: "While the Secretariat is unable to advise on recourse available to someone who has concerns about the institutional processes for research that is not funded by the Agencies, we expect that other avenues may be available, for example, via legal proceedings." In other words, as Leo summarized, "if someone has a complaint about a privately funded study, they should complain to the organization that did the research. Failing that, they can take the research institution to court."

It is ridiculous to expect anyone, especially the parents and guardians of the children harmed in the Prince Albert School Study, to have the financial means to take a Canadian university to court. As my colleague Martin Letendre stated to Leo in an interview for his article, "Legal recourses and civil courts are not the solution to protect research participants. It's absurd."[6] In the current system, egregious violations of research participants' rights, safety, and welfare like those that occurred in the Prince Albert School Study go unchecked, and once revealed and reported, go uninvestigated.

DR. ROGER POISSON

A whole-hearted attempt to create a good and ethical system of human research governance was initiated in Canada over twenty years ago, incited by the questionable research practices of a Montreal surgeon, Dr. Roger Poisson.

Dr. Poisson immigrated to Canada from France in 1952, when he was twenty-one years old. He earned a medical degree from the University of Ottawa and a specialty in surgery from McGill University. For forty-five years, Dr. Poisson practised surgery at Saint-Luc Hospital in Montreal. In 1980, he joined over five thousand other doctors from five hundred institutions across North America in the prestigious National Surgical Adjuvant Breast and Bowel Project. During his association with the project, Dr. Poisson actively participated in fourteen clinical trials and was a prolific contributor, enroling over fifteen hundred research participants, the majority of which were his breast cancer patients. Over Dr. Poisson's tenure in the project, Saint-Luc Hospital received more than one million U.S. dollars in support from the National Cancer Institute of the United States.[7]

Dr. Ann Brown was a biostatistician working on the project. On a hot summer day in 1990, as she scoured over the study data, she noticed something odd in the documents from Dr. Poisson's study site. One of Dr. Poisson's research participants had two different surgery dates for the same cancer, and depending on which date was correct, this individual may not have been eligible to participate in the study. This discrepancy raised concerns within the project. In September 1990, project officials conducted an audit of Dr. Poisson's Montreal study site to assuage its concerns.

Dr. Brown's innocuous discovery proved to be the thin edge of the wedge of a deliberate fraud committed by Dr. Poisson. The audit revealed various discrepancies in Dr. Poisson's records, including irregularities in the informed consent forms. The most striking observation was that Dr. Poisson had been keeping two sets of study data. On one set he appended a yellow sticky note with the French word *vrai*, or true. The other set he labelled *faux*, or false.

Without mentioning their findings to Dr. Poisson, the project's officials reported them to regulatory offices in the United States, including the National Cancer Institute and the Office of Scientific Integrity (now known as the Office of Research Integrity).

The Office of Scientific Integrity launched its own investigation in 1992. It examined 1,054 of Dr. Poisson's case files and found 115 incidents of fraud affecting ninety-nine research participants. Dr. Poisson had been falsifying records throughout his association with the project. He would alter a patient's medical file to change the date of their biopsy or cancer surgery in an attempt to meet certain trial entry criteria, and surprisingly, he did not alter the data thereafter. In one case, in order to enrol a patient in a study, he disguised the fact that she had cancer in both breasts to circumvent the eligibility criterion that only one breast be affected. To hide this fabrication, Dr. Poisson withheld radiation treatment from the non-study breast. In another case, he concealed a patient's history of congestive heart failure and then entered her into a study of a drug that was potentially toxic to the heart. He also entered a patient into a study who had advanced cancer even though the study was designed for patients with earlier stages of cancer.

The Office of Scientific Integrity released the report of its investigation in February 1993, but the media would not catch wind of it until almost a year later. On March 13, 1994, a scathing report of Dr. Poisson and his affiliation with the project made the front page of the *Chicago Tribune*, precipitating a wave of media reports throughout North America. The National Cancer Institute immediately launched a sweeping audit of all of the project's clinical trial sites, including other sites in Montreal. It found a small number of ineligible patients at two other participating hospitals in Montreal: Saint Mary's Hospital and the Jewish General Hospital. These findings and others led to the firing of the project's director and threatened the future of the project altogether.

THE DESCHAMPS REPORT
On May 30, 1995, the United States government sued Saint-Luc Hospital for US$518,175 (approximately $725,445 in Canadian

dollars at the time) "for costs the United States incurred to investigate and eliminate false data a cancer surgeon at the hospital submitted in an international study of breast cancer funded through the National Institutes of Health."[8] The Quebec government responded to the newsworthy saga of Dr. Poisson and the pending lawsuit by mandating the provincial minister of health and social services, Lucienne Robillard, to conduct a formal review with a committee of experts. A committee was created and commissioned to analyze the current status of clinical research in Quebec's public sector and make recommendations to improve the quality of the research conducted, the integrity of the researchers involved, and the safety of research participants. The main goal of the review was to regain the public's trust in Quebec's health research sector.

The committee was given a meagre operating budget of $29,900 to cover honoraria for its three members, their travel expenses, and the costs of producing its report. The committee members included Pierre Deschamps, a lawyer and adjunct professor in the Faculty of Law at McGill University; Dr. Sylvia Cruess, an endocrinologist and associate professor in the Faculty of Medicine at McGill University; and Dr. Patrick Vinay, a nephrologist and dean of the Faculty of Medicine at the Université de Montréal. The committee's report was published in French in 1995, and then in English in 1998 under the title *Report on Control Mechanisms for Clinical Research in Québec*, or as it is more commonly known, the Deschamps Report.[9]

The Deschamps Report proposed a workable institutional framework for health-care research, replete with mechanisms for operating and evaluating research studies scientifically, ethically, and financially. Among other elements in the proposal, the report elucidated that for an institution to operate effectively, it needed to be capable of training research staff, managing human resources, overseeing the quality of its research, improving its conduct, managing contracts with sponsors and others, and overseeing the allocated funds. It recommended that the Quebec government create a monitoring structure to oversee health-care research in the province to ensure that "each and every investigator, institution and developer assume their responsibilities in order to ensure the appropriate carrying out and the proper evaluation of research activities."

"IS ANYBODY MINDING THE STORE?"

Most importantly, the Deschamps Report introduced the concept that the protection of human research participants is a shared responsibility. This was a pivotal shift in thinking at a time when the research community perceived research ethics boards to be the sole protectors of research participants' rights, safety, and welfare. Dr. Michael McDonald described this misconception in his paper "Canadian Governance of Health Research Involving Human Subjects: Is Anybody Minding the Store?" He stated that "all the major actors (including research sponsors, institutions, and regulators) behave as if REB [research ethics board] approval is all that there is to the ethical conduct of research involving human subjects. The REB process (and with it the focus on the research proposal and the consent form) has become the reification of the sum total of responsibilities and accountabilities for researchers, research institutions, research sponsors, and research regulators. In effect, this rationalizes the avoidance of major responsibilities that arise before, after and on the peripheries of the REB review process."[10]

The Deschamps Report helped us to understand that the responsibility for safeguarding the rights, safety, and welfare of research participants is shared among all individuals that interact, directly or indirectly, with research participants, including the investigator and research staff, the institution and its research ethics board, and the sponsors or funders of the research. This concept bestows important functions and powers associated with the research on all players involved.

THE NATIONAL COUNCIL ON ETHICS IN HUMAN RESEARCH

The 1980s witnessed a shift in the placement of privately funded health research from the public sector to the private sector. In other words, health research funded by drug companies and other private sponsors was moving from Canadian institutions, like hospitals and universities, to physicians practising medicine in the community. This development concerned the Medical Research Council of Canada because its influence was confined to research conducted in publicly funded institutions. As research moved from the institutions to the community, the Medical Research Council would become less effective at ensuring the ethical conduct of research through its Canadian Guideline, which I introduced in chapter 7. In 1989, to address this shortcoming, the Medical Research Council of Canada, Health Canada, and the Royal College of Physicians and Surgeons of Canada funded the formation of a new entity called the National Council on Bioethics in Human Research. This organization would later change its name to the National Council on Ethics in Human Research, or NCEHR as it was commonly known (I will refer to it as the National Council).

The National Council was incorporated as a non-profit, independent (non-governmental) organization, and its mission, over its twenty-year existence, was to advance the protection and well-being of human research participants and foster high ethical standards for the conduct of human research. Its activities were administered by a small group of individuals from both the public and private sectors who, along with its funders, participated in its coordinating committee. It implemented numerous well-designed strategies to achieve its goals, including a voluntary oversight service for public institutions that desired an objective evaluation of how closely their procedures aligned with the Canadian Guideline and, eventually, the Policy Statement. The evaluation included an on-site, multi-day visit from the National Council's reviewers that resulted in a series of recommendations for the institution, its authorities, and the research ethics board. These recommendations could be followed to heighten the quality of the institution's operations and enhance the protection of research participants. To complement the evaluation program, the National Council developed educational programs and workshops routinely held across the country.

The National Council sponsored an email platform where research ethics issues could be discussed in an open and collaborative way. Every year, the council brought together research ethicists, bioethicists, research ethics board members, researchers, regulators, policy-makers, sponsors, and funders at its national conference on research ethics. The tremendous value that the email platform and the national conference provided to the research ethics community would be realized only after the National Council was dismantled.

To ensure that we were operating our research ethics board according to the highest ethical standards, we invited the National Council to our offices to conduct an evaluation. The council agreed, making this its first evaluation of a private organization. Three site reviewers, including Pierre Deschamps, visited us for two days in February 2005. At the end of the evaluation, they praised us for the rigour, efficiency, integrity, accountability, and transparency of our ethics review processes, as well as for the qualifications and expertise of our research ethics board members. The conduct of our private research ethics board had far exceeded their expectations and had surpassed that of any public institution they had evaluated before us. Needless to say, we were thrilled with these results.

In April 2005, a task force established by the National Council drafted a report entitled *Options for the Development of an Accreditation System for Human Research Protection Programs* (which I will refer to as the Accreditation Proposal). Pierre Deschamps was one of its authors, so it was not surprising that it espoused the Deschamps Report by stressing the shared responsibility for research participant protection. This concept was manifested in the first element of the Accreditation Proposal in that organizations conducting or overseeing research on humans were expected to establish a Human Research Protection Program or HRPP (I will refer to it as a Protection Program). The authors of the Accreditation Proposal introduced the concept of a Protection Program using the definition from a 2002 report of the United States Institute of Medicine entitled *Responsible Research: A Systems Approach to Protecting Research Participants*: "a system composed of interdependent elements that come together to implement policies and practices that ensure appropriate protection of research participants." Within the definition, the basic protection functions included the "comprehensive review of protocols (including scientific, financial conflict of interest, and ethical reviews); ethically sound participant-investigator interactions; on-going and risk-appropriate safety monitoring; and quality improvement and compliance activities." The U.S. report stated that for a Protection Program to be effective, it needed to operate within an environment that included measures for internal auditing or accountability, adequate resources for its research and oversight activities, training programs for those involved in the conduct and oversight of human research, and open communication and interaction with all stakeholders in the research enterprise.

The Accreditation Proposal argued that the Protection Programs developed by organizations should be accredited to ensure that they applied the contemplated accreditation standards consistently. The standards would be rooted in the Policy Statement and existing federal, provincial, and territorial laws, regulations, and policies. The Accreditation Proposal also described various options regarding the structure of the accrediting body, the development and maintenance of standards, and the funding of the accreditation program.

The most logical options proposed were that the accrediting body be an entity independent from government, that the accreditation standards be developed by a professional standards development organization, and that funding for the accreditation program come from the applicants for accreditation, with perhaps operational funds from the government.

It goes without saying that we wanted ours to be the first Protection Program accredited in Canada. The United States had already had such a program operating since 2002, but to have an opportunity to be accredited within our own country would have been phenomenal. We pursued the National Council for information on when the program might be launched, and even attended its national conference in the fall of 2005 in anticipation of an announcement. Like many other attendees, we left the meeting disillusioned by the council's evasiveness regarding this critical issue.

THE AMERICAN ACCREDITATION PROGRAM
The National Council's silence regarding the proposed accreditation program was deafening. Apart from feeling betrayed, we were extremely discouraged by Canada's lack of commitment to addressing its issues surrounding human research participant protection. In December 2005, after much reflection on the events we had experienced throughout the year, and unwilling to wait for Canada to embrace accreditation, we made a bold decision to focus our resources on a year-long journey to attain accreditation from the United States.

The Association for the Accreditation of Human Research Protection Programs (the American Accreditation Program) was incorporated in Maryland in 2001 as a non-profit, independent accrediting body for Protection Programs. It was officially launched in 2002, and within one year, six of its founding members had achieved accreditation of their Protection Programs. Our accreditation followed in 2006 at which time we shared the stage with approximately ninety other accredited Protection Programs. We were the second organization to be accredited outside the United States, the first to be accredited in Canada, and the first contract research company accredited in the world.

News of our accreditation sent ripples through the research community. Kudos flowed in from other accredited organizations, and many of the authors of the Accreditation Proposal sent their good wishes to us publicly via the research ethics email platform. The English and French newspapers in Montreal reported on our accreditation, and the news quickly spread throughout the country. In their reports the newspapers positioned us among the ranks of other notable institutions with accredited Protection Programs, like Johns Hopkins Medicine, Harvard University, Yale University, and Stanford University. We received a flood of requests for partnerships from accredited organizations in the United States.

Prior to our accreditation, research ethics boards outside Canada were prohibited from conducting reviews of research that involved Canadians unless the majority of the members of their review quorum were Canadian citizens or permanent residents. Because our operating procedures had been developed according to the same standards as all other accredited Protection Programs, it was easy for us to harmonize our practices and work together. Partnership meant that only one full study review in either country was necessary, with each research ethics board maintaining responsibility over the specific needs of the study sites in their respective country. These partnerships provided, for the first time, a North American solution to cross-border research ethics review. We were surprised to see that, within the first year of our accreditation, the revenues generated from these partnerships more than paid for the costs to get there.

We were baffled by the silence of our federal government, though. It was as if achieving the highest standards in the world

for safeguarding the rights, safety, and welfare of research participants and research quality was commonplace and unworthy of acknowledgement. Referring to the difference in the acceptance of
our accreditation between the United States and Canada, my colleague Martin Letendre mused, "We just became the Céline Dion
of Protection Programs."

THE SPONSORS' TABLE

What we didn't know about the National Council's Accreditation
Proposal was what was going on behind the scenes. In June 2005
the National Council had called a meeting of its funders to review
the public's comments on the Accreditation Proposal and determine the path for the implementation of its recommendations. In
a strange turn of events, in September 2005 the Royal College of
Physicians and Surgeons convened a meeting of stakeholders that
included Health Canada, the three federal research funding agencies, and the Association of Universities and Colleges of Canada
(now known as Universities Canada). The rationale for that meeting was to discuss alternatives to the Accreditation Proposal, which
they alleged was taking too long to come to fruition. The meeting
participants called themselves the Sponsors' Table and subsequently added other Canadian organizations to the mix. At this meeting, the participants agreed to establish the Experts Committee
for Human Research Participant Protection in Canada (which I
will refer to as the Experts Committee) to investigate governance
models for the oversight of human research, such as accreditation,
and explore implementation and funding options. If this sounds
familiar, it's because this is exactly what the National Council had
just proposed. Why the Sponsors' Table thought it was necessary
to re-examine the issue is unknown.

It took two years and an undisclosed amount of taxpayer funds
for the Experts Committee to publish its report, which it called

Moving Ahead. The *Moving Ahead* report was remarkably congruent to the Accreditation Proposal. One minor difference between them was the terminology used for the Protection Programs. The Accreditation Proposal used the international term "Human Research Protection Programs," or HRPP, whereas *Moving Ahead* called it "Programs for Ensuring Ethical Research with Humans," or PEERH.

The *Moving Ahead* report reflected on the costs and time frame required to implement its recommendations. It concluded that an annual budget of nine to ten million dollars and a fifty-one-person staff would be required for the accrediting body to be operational, and that it would take three years to establish. In an attempt to temper the anticipated negative reaction to the high costs proposed in the *Moving Ahead* report, a small paragraph was inserted on page 85. The authors opined that the government could save two million dollars annually by dismantling the beloved National Council and the newly formed Interagency Advisory Panel on Research Ethics and transferring their functions to the proposed accrediting body.

The lack of appetite for such a costly accreditation program was probably its Achilles' heel, and we as a country never "moved ahead" with the Experts Committee's proposal. In a shocking twist, and without any prior notice, the National Council lost the remaining bit of funding it had and was forced to close its doors in 2010.[11]

SOBER SECOND THOUGHT

In 2011, the Canadian Senate weighed in on the topic of accreditation. That year it authorized the Senate Standing Committee on Social Affairs, Science and Technology to undertake a study on various issues related to prescription drugs in Canada. Among these were issues concerning clinical trials, including the process of approval by research ethics boards. The results of the study were published in 2012 in a report called *Canada's Clinical Trial*

Infrastructure: A Prescription for Improved Access to New Medicines.
In the report, the committee called upon the federal government to
bring the requirements and obligations surrounding clinical trials
in line with other countries.

The Senate committee recommended that national standards
be developed for all aspects of clinical trials. To ensure conformity
to these standards, it recommended that an accreditation program,
like the one recommended in the *Moving Ahead* report, be created.
In the report the committee wrote, "In order to ensure that all
clinical trials of unapproved drugs are reviewed in a consistent and
efficient manner, adoption of a national standard can be ensured
through an accreditation program, as has previously been recommended in the *Moving Ahead* report of 2008." The committee concluded by stating that "once comprehensive standards for clinical
trials and compulsory accreditation of research ethics boards are
implemented, the committee is confident that the number of clinical trials conducted in Canada will increase."[12]

Around the same time as the Senate committee's report was
published, a group of Canadian research ethicists and researchers published the paper "Research Ethics Broadly Writ: Beyond
REB Review."[13] The authors highlighted the ethical implications
of human research that reside outside the mandate of the research
ethics board. They warned that, with the demise of the National
Council, Canada's governance system had no mechanism to address
and oversee ethical issues that did not fall under the research ethics
board's purview: "Now that NCEHR has ceased its activities, there
is a gaping hole in Canada's research ethics governance system. This
means that many of the broader (extra-REB) ethical issues remain
unaddressed by our current governance system, creating conditions
ripe for institutional failure." The authors recommended that a national system of accreditation for human research be developed to
address this gap in governance: "Broader recognition of the wide

scope of research ethics is required, along with a more systematic approach to dealing with the whole spectrum of ethical issues involved. Of paramount importance is the creation of a national body charged with establishing and overseeing a shared vision of research ethics governance via the accreditation and monitoring of institutions conducting research involving human subjects."

NATIONAL STANDARD OF CANADA

Following the Senate committee's call for national standards, Health Canada assumed the mantle and commissioned the Canadian General Standards Board (CGSB) to develop a national standard for research ethics review. In a personal communication with the CGSB, I learned that Health Canada had paid the standards board three hundred thousand dollars to develop the standard.

The CGSB is a Crown corporation accredited by the Standards Council of Canada and as such, was required to adhere to strict criteria in the development of its standards. In 2013, the CGSB published a national standard of Canada entitled *Research Ethics Oversight of Biomedical Clinical Trials*. During the development of the standard and shortly after its publication, some members of the technical committee voiced their dissatisfaction with the development process. Other members quit the technical committee altogether following contentious disagreements regarding the standard's content. While disagreement is expected during the process of developing standards, the leaders of the technical committee must ensure that decisions accommodate all members' opinions through the compulsory process of consensus decision-making.

An additional point of contention came from users of the standard. In order to obtain a copy of the standard, a fee had to be paid to the CGSB. This insulted users. They felt that the standard should have been provided free of charge since Health Canada had already paid the CGSB, using taxpayer dollars, to develop it. The acrimony created during the development process and after publication led to the withdrawal of the national standard from publication. This was a very unfortunate outcome. The national standard might not have been acceptable to everyone, but it was the first one to be published for human research, and it was a solid foundation from which other standards could be developed in the future.

The Canadian government spent hundreds of thousands, maybe millions, of dollars developing reports to address ways to improve the governance of human research. Over a span of eight years, we observed the publication of the Accreditation Proposal, the *Moving Ahead* report, the Senate committee's report, and the national standard on research ethics review, only to see all of these efforts sidelined.

With the National Council all but a memory, the Secretariat on Responsible Conduct of Research and its associated panels became the quintessential arbiters of all things related to human research ethics in Canada. From them we would never hear about accountability, transparency, accreditation, or any other efforts to create a good and ethical governance system for human research.

10

GOOD AND ETHICAL GOVERNANCE, PART II

UNDETECTED ≠ NON-EXISTENT

Time continued to pass, and no further efforts were made toward a better system of human research governance in Canada. By 2017, my company's Protection Program had already been accredited south of the border for eleven years. As one of the only leaders of an accredited Protection Program in Canada, I felt that I was uniquely qualified to champion its benefits. My advocacy for accreditation and the protection of research participants' rights, safety, and welfare became a mainstay of my presentations at industry meetings.

But the reception was usually mixed. There were those who applauded a better system of oversight and accountability and those who simply stared back at me. I knew exactly what those stares meant: "What is Janice talking about?" "Why is she rocking the boat?" "We don't need any more regulations!" "The system is working fine." "I would have heard if there were problems."

The sad truth is that when a system of governance fails to assess compliance through an objective oversight program, those within the system are left with a false sense of security. They're under the illusion that the system is running smoothly and that no changes are needed to make it better. They consider media reports about human research tragedies, like the Prince Albert School Study, which we saw in chapter 8, and the Montreal pediatric oncology study, which I discuss in this chapter, as singular and often sensationalized events.

My colleagues and I understood the assurances that an accredited Protection Program would provide for all stakeholders of human research. What confused us was why such a simple solution was being ignored.

BENEFITS OF A PROTECTION PROGRAM

As presented in the last chapter, the general framework of a Protection Program was first introduced by Pierre Deschamps in 1995. It was adopted by the American Accreditation Program and was subsequently recommended in the reports by the National Council and the Experts Committee.

A Protection Program is not a static entity. It is a dynamic program with a proper governance structure that includes effective leadership, rigorous operating procedures, resources and funding that meet the volume and complexity of the research undertaken, ongoing training of staff, and quality assurance to monitor research practices and recommend changes for improvement.

A Protection Program places the interests of the research participants and the integrity of the research data at the heart of its mission. Because research participant protection is a shared responsibility, the Protection Program includes all of the individuals and departments whose actions directly or indirectly affect the research data and the health, welfare, interests, and rights of research participants. For example, a Protection Program in a hospital would include the leadership of the research enterprise; the researchers and research staff; the research ethics board and its administration; specific departments that provide support to the research such as the pharmacy, laboratory, imaging, biosafety, and privacy and contracts offices; and administrative and ancillary personnel.

For the organization with a Protection Program, accreditation promotes a culture of responsible conduct of research. It assures the organization that its procedures meet or exceed all ethical and regulatory requirements, leading to increased efficiencies that are documented and translated into practice. And most of all, it promotes a risk-reduction consciousness that results in a safer environment for research participants. Accreditation also creates a harmonized research landscape, as organizations with accredited Protection Programs all operate according to procedures developed to conform with the same standards.

For the public, accreditation provides assurances that safeguards are in place to protect their rights, safety, and welfare when they choose to participate in research. It also promotes the public's trust in researchers and confidence in the data they produce.

THE MONTREAL PEDIATRIC ONCOLOGY STUDY

For sponsors and funders of Canadian research, accreditation would provide an objective assessment of a funding applicant's proven ability to follow the Policy Statement, especially with respect to safeguarding the rights, safety, and welfare of research participants.

In reviewing applications for Canadian research funding, the three federal research funding agencies employ the expertise of independent evaluators, who consider specific criteria in their evaluation of human research, including its potential impact on the current state of knowledge. Incredibly, there are no data to indicate that the evaluators consider Health Canada's inspection reports in their funding recommendations.

Consider the fate of six children who were recruited to participate in a clinical trial at Montreal's Sainte-Justine University Hospital Centre in 2015. Dr. Henrique Bittencourt, a pediatric hematologist and oncologist at the hospital, was the principal investigator of the study. After obtaining funding and the appropriate institutional approvals from the hospital, Dr. Bittencourt, together with other investigators at the hospital, embarked on a clinical trial in children with leukemias and solid tumours. The trial involved a combination of two drugs: the epigenetic drug decitabine and an isoflavone called genistein. In the first phase of the trial, the maximum tolerated dose of the drug combination would be evaluated. The second phase would determine the efficacy and safety of that maximum tolerated dose.

A few months into the first phase of the trial, the research staff noticed numerous inconsistencies in the way the study was being conducted. One of these was the infusion of expired drug into the children, something that the research staff alerted Dr. Bittencourt to, but he brazenly continued the infusions regardless. Research staff tried, without success, to correct these issues by bringing them to the attention of their superiors and other departments within the hospital. When they failed to get anyone to pay attention to them, they launched an anonymous complaint with Health Canada and later leaked the story to investigative journalists at CBC/Radio-Canada.

The Health Canada Inspectorate conducted an inspection of the clinical trial and suspended it in November 2016. In its initial report, the Inspectorate observed seventy-six violations of the Food and Drugs Act, including twenty-three critical infractions that threatened the health and safety of the children participating in the trial.[1]

Dr. Bittencourt and his team also breached the ethical principles of the Policy Statement. However, since the elements of the

Policy Statement were beyond the scope of the Inspectorate's mandate, these breaches were not revealed in the Inspectorate's report. But they were revealed through the hard work of Pasquale Turbide, an investigative journalist at CBC/Radio-Canada.[2]

Because the research participants were children, consent to participate in the clinical trial was solicited from their parents by Dr. Bittencourt and the other study investigators, who were also the children's doctors. This produced a situation where the investigators unduly influenced the parents' decisions. The parents were also experiencing the unimaginable stress inherent in having a terminally ill child for whom no other treatment options were available.

Deeply troubling was that the information conveyed to the parents by the investigators was done in haste and was misleading, exaggerated, and in some cases wrong. For example, the parents were told that their children would achieve remission in the clinical trial even though the possibility of remission was an experimental outcome of the study.

For parents of a child with cancer, "remission" is the buzzword that gives them hope and strongly influences their decision to consent to study participation. In the words of one parent, "You have to hope for a cure or pray to heaven. When you're in that void, you're trying to grab on to whatever you can — and that was the study."[3] In their solicitation the researchers breached the two main elements of informed consent: that it be informed and provided freely. Rushing the process of consent, or treating it as a perfunctory routine, violated the ethical principle of respect for persons in the context of informed consent.

A few years after this research project was shut down by Health Canada, Dr. Bittencourt and his colleagues received grants of over one million dollars from one of the federal research funding agencies to further their research in pediatric cancers.[4] It was clear that the funding agency did not consider the Inspectorate's report about the pediatric oncology study in its decision to continue to fund Dr. Bittencourt's research interests. Moreover, when it came to the assurances that an accreditation program could offer them, as we will see in the next chapter, the federal research funding agencies ignored and stifled recommendations for accreditation and went about their business distributing millions of taxpayer dollars annually to researchers without any guardrails.

ANIMAL PROTECTION > HUMAN PROTECTION

It may be surprising to learn that the federal research funding agencies observe and support a program of objective oversight for animal research through the Canadian Council on Animal Care and have been doing so for almost forty years.[5] So why have they not adopted an equivalent system for human research?

The Canadian Council on Animal Care was founded in 1968 as an affiliated committee of the Association of Universities and Colleges of Canada. In 1982, it was incorporated as an independent (non-government) non-profit organization. Its mission was, and still is, to ensure that animal research is conducted only when it is necessary and is performed in accordance with the highest standards of ethics and care. It accomplishes this through the development of research-based standards in collaboration with Canadian stakeholders, as well as through a complementary program of oversight to ensure that these standards are being met. Institutions that conduct animal research in conformity with the standards are awarded a Certificate of Good Animal Practice.[6]

Funding for the Canadian Council on Animal Care comes from two sources. Its operating funds are supplied by two of the three federal research funding agencies, and additional funding is contributed by its certified organizations through annual program fees. Since 1986, Good Animal Practice certification has been mandatory for any researcher from an eligible organization who is applying for federal funding to conduct animal research.[7]

Through the Canadian Council on Animal Care's independent assessments, the federal research funding agencies can objectively assess the quality of conduct of the funding applicants and be assured of the safety and well-being of the animals in the research that they fund. Consequently, the Canadian public can trust the federal research funding agencies' decisions to fund specific animal research projects. As described in the previous chapter, this is the system of governance that the National Council and the Experts Committee were proposing to emulate for human research.

As a result of the Canadian Council on Animal Care's certification program, an animal researcher's conduct is continuously monitored. Researchers are accountable for their actions and make conscious decisions to follow procedures. But what influences these decisions? Through a psychological phenomenon called the Hawthorne effect, we modify our behaviour when we are aware that we are being watched. This phenomenon gets its name from a series of experiments carried out in the 1920s and 1930s by an electrical company outside Chicago called the Hawthorne Works. The goal of the experiments was to understand how changes in the work environment, such as changing the lighting or the length of the workday, affected the productivity of the employees.

At first glance, the results of the experiments were unremarkable, and the company found no use for them. Years later, a researcher by the name of Henry Landsberger revisited the experimental data and discovered that employee productivity increased briefly any time a change in the workplace was introduced. For example, productivity increased when the lights were brightened, but also when they were dimmed. Similar results were observed both when the length of the workday was decreased and when it was increased. Landsberger discovered that the only constant in these experiments to explain the increased productivity was the presence of individuals measuring that productivity. Landsberger concluded that the increased levels of productivity were unrelated to changes in the workplace. Rather, the employees were more productive when they were being watched. Today, the Hawthorne effect is also called the observer effect or viewing effect.

But is the opposite true? Do we change our behaviour when we know that we are *not* being watched? It is possible that Dr. Bittencourt and his team knew that their adherence to the ethical principles of the Policy Statement were not being monitored. Did they know that they would not suffer any consequences for exaggerating the benefits of the clinical trial or for putting enormous pressure on the parents to consent to their children's participation? Did they know that knowledge of their serious ethical breaches would never make their way to the federal research funding agencies?

The six children recruited into the pediatric oncology study spent a large portion of their last days in a clinical trial that, because of how it was conducted, had no chance of benefitting them or any future patients like them. Who was protecting these children? It certainly wasn't Dr. Bittencourt, although by law it was his responsibility to do so. It didn't seem to be the institution, since complaints by the research staff to various institutional departments went unanswered. It didn't seem to be Health Canada through its inspection process, even though its website claims to ensure the protection of research participants. And it wasn't the federal research funding agencies because, as we learned from the Prince Albert School Study, oversight by the Secretariat is limited only to studies funded by the agencies. The protection of the children's rights, safety, and welfare was an illusion.

CHAMPIONING THE CAUSE

At a loss to explain the government's reluctance to create a functional governance system for human research, I read and reread the reports presented by the National Council and the Experts Committee. I compared their recommendations to the features of the American Accreditation Program, the Canadian Council on Animal Care's certification program, and the accreditation program for health care provided by Accreditation Canada. I identified their common strengths while taking careful note of any weaknesses. Then I began mapping out what an optimal Canadian accreditation program for human research would look like.

The idea of developing a Canadian accreditation program began as a casual conversation I had with my business partners. It didn't take long before we started seriously discussing how we could do it without jeopardizing our ongoing responsibilities to our businesses. We worked out a solution, and in the fall of 2017, I resigned as president of my operating companies and transferred my duties and responsibilities to others. Free of competing obligations, I was able to devote all of my time to developing the accreditation program. Needless to say, I wouldn't have been able to embark on this challenging initiative without the support and understanding of my business partners.

Recall that the Experts Committee's *Moving Ahead* report proposed that it would take a staff of fifty-one and an annual budget of nine to ten million dollars to establish a Canadian accreditation program. It also estimated that it would take three years for the program to be operational. It would have been foolish to think that I could do the work of fifty-one people by myself, and I only had the budget to hire one full-time person to help me get the program off the ground. We were told that we were not eligible for funding from the federal research funding agencies, which we found confusing since it was pouring millions of taxpayer dollars into the operations of the Canadian Council on Animal Care every year. We incorporated our company in an identical manner to the animal council and could have argued this point with the government, but we decided to spend our time seeking funds from private sources.

The stars aligned the day that I met Clarissa Alberti Fleck, who had recently graduated with a degree in biology from McGill University. Her intelligence and positive disposition, mixed with the perfect amount of moxie, were just what our accreditation initiative needed. Clarissa was cheerful and outgoing, and as an added bonus, she brought humour to our longest and most difficult days. She was a quick study and soon became fluent in the specifics of our accreditation program. It took no time for her to embrace our mission and become passionate about our work.

Clarissa and I prepared the foundation for the accreditation program. We chose the descriptive name "Human Research Accreditation Canada" (HRA Canada) to define us corporately, and we used the constellation Orion to symbolize our mission of protecting or shielding research participants from harm.

Our work began with the arduous task of writing operating procedures for the program's administration, then moved on to the other operational layers, such as the site reviewers and accreditation council. Since we were at least two years away from developing national standards for human research, we based the accreditation program on internal standards. With the help of external experts, the accreditation council developed internal standards replete with the requirements for a Protection Program and two of its components, the research ethics board and the conduct of human research. Each requirement was painstakingly cross-referenced to the relevant Canadian and United States laws and regulations, the Policy Statement, and the Good Clinical Practice Guideline.

By the first week of January 2018, we were ready to introduce HRA Canada to the Canadian research community. We released posts on LinkedIn and Twitter promoting the importance of a Protection Program and the benefits of its accreditation. We requested that anyone interested in volunteering in the initiative contact us. The responses to our posts were overwhelming. One particular response captured our attention: "It is very exciting news and I would definitely be interested in considering being a member of the accrediting council. As you know, this is something I have long been advocating so this is fantastic. Please let me know more about the initiative." This response came from Alexander Karabanow.

I first met Alex when he was the president of the Canadian Association of Research Ethics Boards, an association I'll talk more about in the next chapter. At the time we were launching our accreditation program, Alex was managing clinical research services operations at the University Health Network in Toronto and was instrumental in designing its institutional authorization model for research, a program that resembles, in some respects, a Protection Program.

Alex's mind was a steel trap when it came to the history of research ethics and the institutions and individuals involved. His superpower was his sincere and engaging personality; it seemed like he was connected to virtually everyone in the human research and research ethics world within two or three degrees of separation.

I recall a meeting that Alex and I had at Ryerson University (now renamed Toronto Metropolitan University). Ten years earlier, Alex had coordinated the human and animal research ethics activities there. Our meeting was with the management of the university's research ethics board and our objective was to introduce them to the HRA Canada accreditation program. While we sat in the reception area awaiting our meeting, people from all over started pouring in to greet Alex. It was as if Ryerson had announced "Alex is in the building!" Each person that approached him said, "I heard you were here. I just had to come and see you." I felt so fortunate to work alongside him and to be exposed to all of the incredible people in his circle.

Alex became the inaugural chair of HRA Canada's accreditation council and quickly brought to the council a stellar group of individuals from across the country. Like Alex, the council members were passionate about creating a system of oversight for human research through accreditation. Jacquelyn Legere was one such member.

When I first met Jacquelyn, she was in the process of spearheading the formation of a Protection Program at Horizon Health Network, the largest public health network in New Brunswick. The first things I noticed about Jacquelyn were her pragmatic sensibility and her diplomacy. Like Alex, Jacquelyn's depth of knowledge of research ethics was boundless. Together, they ensured that the accreditation council's assessments were achieved through the council members' consensus agreement after a thorough and objective review.

For an applicant's Protection Program to attain accreditation by HRA Canada, its written procedures needed to be assessed to ensure that they conformed to the accreditation standards. Once accredited, the applicant's Protection Program would undergo yearly assessments to ensure that its practices complied with its accredited procedures. The individuals who conduct these assessments are called site reviewers.

HRA Canada's site reviewers were chosen based on their expertise, experience, and diplomacy. Diplomacy was an important and necessary criterion in our choice of site reviewers because we wholeheartedly believed that accreditation was a journey and not an endpoint and that every assessment the site reviewers conducted was a learning experience for the accredited organization.

Last, but certainly not least, HRA Canada needed an advisory board that could set the objectives for the accreditation program and regularly review and revise them. Without a hint of hesitation, three former members of the National Council and pioneers of accreditation, Pierre Deschamps, Dr. Michael McDonald, and Dr. Michael Owen, accepted the responsibility to oversee our initiative as advisory board members.

ACCREDITATION STANDARDS

The Policy Statement has been wrongly described as a Canadian standard. It is not a standard; rather, it is a policy of the federal research funding agencies. A policy should describe which specific concepts are important and answer the question "Why do I need to do this?"

A standard, on the other hand, assigns quantifiable measures to a policy and answers the question "What is required in order to do this?" A standard is expressed in the form of requirements. Based on the requirements, procedures can be developed that establish the proper steps to take to conform to the policy. A standard doesn't replace a policy or diminish its importance. On the contrary, a standard eliminates the variability in interpreting policies and other regulatory and guidance documents, and it provides clear, concise requirements upon which procedures can be developed.

To illustrate the interplay between a policy and a standard, let's think back to the early days of the Covid-19 pandemic. We were told that physical distancing was important to reduce the transmission of disease. This policy did its job: It conveyed what was important and why. Experts in public safety and epidemiology quickly assigned a quantifiable measure to this policy. They determined that, to meet the policy, we must keep a distance of two metres, or the length of one hockey stick, apart. Once we knew the standard to apply, it was easy to establish procedures for our work and everyday life, such as how far to stand behind someone at a grocery store checkout counter.

By the fall of 2019, HRA Canada was ready to replace its internal accreditation standards with Canadian national standards.

Although our internal standards were comprehensive and well-written, they were not developed through the consensus agreement of stakeholders across the country.

The only entities in Canada qualified to develop national standards are standards development organizations accredited by the Standards Council of Canada. In September 2019 I met with the standards council at its head office in Ottawa to gather information on what was entailed in the standards development organization accreditation program. After considering all of our options, we got to work to form a standards development organization and achieve accreditation so that we could develop national standards for human research.

It was recommended that we incorporate a new entity for the standards development organization to keep it at arm's length from HRA Canada, our accrediting body for Protection Programs. This made perfect sense to us, and we quickly filed the incorporation papers for a new non-government, non-profit company called the Human Research Standards Organization. With Clarissa fully occupied on the accreditation side, I began writing operating procedures that dovetailed with the requirements for accreditation by the Standards Council of Canada.

We were granted our accreditation in February 2020 and immediately got to work. We began by inviting Canadian stakeholders to participate on our first technical committee, which would develop our first foundational national standard, Development of a Human Research Protection Program. Once we had recruited about two dozen trained members and contributors, our newly formed technical committee met, first in May 2020 and then weekly thereafter, to develop the national standard.

As we were all isolating to protect ourselves and others from a deadly virus, our weekly ninety-minute technical committee meetings were a special time to socialize and break the monotony, albeit virtually. We were all Zoom novices and struggled to master new skills like screen sharing, chatting, raising our virtual hands, and unmuting. Our concern for each other's health was evident in the first ten minutes of each meeting. We shared personal stories and updated each other on what we had learned about SARS-CoV-2 testing numbers and Covid-19 hospitalizations and deaths since our last meeting. Toward the end of 2020, my father contracted the virus and was fighting for his life in an intensive care unit, and although I didn't feel comfortable sharing my pain and fear, it comforted me to know that I could.

At our last meeting, we reviewed the numerous comments we'd received from stakeholders and the community during the national standard's sixty-day public consultation period. The national standard was published by the Standards Council of Canada at the end of November 2020, and it was nothing short of a major milestone for Canadian human research. My father passed away a few days later.

We had already begun developing our second national standard, Ethical Review and Oversight of Human Research, with another group of technical committee members at the time that our first national standard was released to stakeholders and the research community for consultation. The second standard concerned the requirements that research ethics boards must conform to when administering their services and conducting their reviews. We celebrated the publication of this national standard in June 2021.

Our third foundational national standard, Conduct of Human Research, was developed by yet another technical committee. It took a bit longer to develop than the previous two, mainly because of its wide scope. This national standard was published in April 2022.

To support the national standards, we developed a global standard concerning the training of stakeholders on human research protection, Development of a Training Program for Human Research Protection. This was published in April 2023.

The Standards Council of Canada did not have a fee structure that encouraged a small company such as the Human Research Standards Organization to maintain its accreditation for the long term. In fact, the Standards Council of Canada's accreditation fees were the same for our organization as they were for established standards development organizations with hundreds of published national standards. Since the Human Research Standards Organization provided its published national standards to consumers free of charge, it didn't have a source of revenue. Somehow, we found the funds necessary to successfully develop the three foundational national standards, but this business model was not sustainable. We subsequently withdrew our accreditation from the Standards Council of Canada and transferred the maintenance of our foundational national standards to our trusted partner, the Digital Governance Standards Institute, an accredited standards development organization founded by Jim Balsillie, the co-founder of Research in Motion. At the time of this writing, we are on the verge of publishing our first joint national standard on the governance of human research data.

KINDRED SPIRITS

In the words of the famous American labour leader and civil rights activist Dolores Huerta, "*Sí, se puede*" ("Yes, we can"). And we did! By uniting stakeholders at the grassroots level from almost every province and territory of Canada, we reached the goals previously set by the National Council and the Experts Committee to develop national standards for human research and an accreditation body for Protection Programs. We worked together, without any political or power aspirations, for the good of human research and in the best interests of human research participants. We developed the oversight that was so badly needed to fix the broken system of human research governance in Canada.

In late 2019, Alex, Clarissa, and I started a LinkedIn Group called Human Research Accreditation and Standards. Alex was by far the most prolific member, posting daily on important contemporary issues related to human research. We also used this platform to announce milestones and news related to HRA Canada and the Human Research Standards Organization, such as the public consultation periods for the national standards we were developing. By 2024, our group had blossomed to five thousand members, the majority of whom were Canadians working within the human research enterprise.

Clarissa had a good understanding of the untapped potential of our websites, so she established analytics to monitor website traffic and the number of downloads of the Human Research Standards Organization's standards. We had a steady stream of visitors to our websites, primarily from Canadian cities, with curiosity also coming from major cities south of the border. By 2024, the Human Research Standards Organization's standards had been downloaded approximately two thousand times. This number may be an underestimate because once a standard was downloaded, we lost the ability to monitor how many times it was shared by the person who downloaded it. Regardless, the national standards were well received by the research community, and we often heard from those who used them that they were valuable in the development of effective operating procedures.

In two short years, the Human Research Standards Organization had held over seventy-five technical committee meetings and united over one thousand stakeholders in the development of Canada's first three foundational national standards for human research. I maintained a list of hundreds of people who requested that I keep their names on file for consideration for future technical committees. The list included individuals who had previously participated in the development of the Human Research Standards Organization's national standards and others who wished to be part of the process. That these people were interested in dedicating their free time to standardizing the Canadian human research landscape was a testament to what we had built and how important it was to the research community.

WE INSPIRED A NATION

The Australian government's Department of Health and Aged Care commissioned a literature review of the standards and accreditation programs existing around the world. The report was published in March 2023 and highlighted the American Accreditation Program, the Health Research Authority's program in England, and HRA Canada's program.[8]

We were proud and a bit overwhelmed to learn that the Australian government's Commission on Safety and Quality in Health Care adopted HRA Canada's accreditation model. At the time of this writing, national standards are currently in development in Australia, upon which an accreditation program will be established.

A NOT SO PRIVY ENDORSEMENT

The Privy Council Office is a department of the Canadian government that supports the prime minister's vision, goals, and decisions. One of the functional units within the Privy Council is the Impact and Innovation Unit. This unit undertakes studies aimed at investigating potential solutions to the country's economic, environmental, and social problems.

In a landmark decision in the fall of 2023, the Impact and Innovation Unit established a precedent by mandating Protection Program accreditation as a crucial requirement for the ethical review of its human research activities. In its request for proposals for research ethics board services, it explicitly required that potential vendors exist within a Protection Program and be in good accreditation standing with either HRA Canada or the American Accreditation Program.

The condition imposed by the Privy Council signified a groundbreaking public acknowledgement of the importance of our accreditation program, affirming its parity with the program in the United States. It also confirmed the value of accreditation and its significance as an objective, independent validation of the quality of an organization's Protection Program. We were thrilled to see our hard work recognized at this level of government — an encouraging moment that stood in stark contrast to what the next chapter reveals.

II

UNSAVOURY HEADWINDS

OVERCOMING THE URGE TO RESIST CHANGE

Humans are innately resistant to change, thanks to a tiny part of the brain called the amygdala. The amygdala participates in the brain's processing of emotions like fear and anxiety and controls how we adapt to change. It interprets change as a threat and protects us from this threat by signalling the release of hormones for the freeze, flight, or fight response. Consequently, our initial reaction to change or to a new idea or initiative is to resist it, despite how good it may be for us.

We were not naive to the fact that we might face resistance to the changes we were proposing, and we understood that we had to present an ironclad argument that would overcome our colleagues' urges to resist these changes. We found that the formula for change published by American organizational theorists Richard Beckhard and Reuben Harris was an interesting way to proceed. The formula, $D \times V \times F > R$, states that for meaningful change to occur in an organization, its members' resistance to a new idea or change (R) must be weaker than the product of their dissatisfaction with the current system (*D*), their vision of a better future (*V*), and the possibility of real and immediate first steps that can be taken to implement the change (*F*).[1]

We set out to prepare a series of presentations, each of which would include the factors for successful change. To meet the "dissatisfaction with the current system" element of the formula, we introduced examples of failures of the current system and the potential harms that it poses to research participants. We knew that how we educated the Canadian human research community would be vital to overcoming the urge to resist change and to moving the country toward a system of good and ethical human research governance.

What we didn't prepare for, however, was that a malicious disinformation campaign would be launched against us. Its objective, it seemed, was to create doubt in our initiative so the status quo could prevail.

For example, neither HRA Canada nor the Human Research Standards Organization had the funding necessary to build an effective education program for our initiative, so we reached out to the Canadian Institutes of Health Research for financial assistance. (By mid-2021, we had already personally invested approximately $750,000 in setting up the corporations and addressing the budget shortfalls experienced in the organizations' day-to-day operations.) We received a positive response from one of the agency's senior advisers. He wrote to the executive director of the Secretariat on Responsible Conduct of Research who maintained funding for such requests, requesting that the Secretariat assist us with our program. We never received a reply to our request for educational funding.

We later learned of the executive director's response through an Access to Information and Privacy request. The executive director wrote, "I do not believe they would qualify [for funding] as nothing in the standard educates users about the TCPS [the Policy Statement].... [I]n my view, support for the promotion of a private initiative runs a risk of creating a precedent.... Happy to discuss." This was such an odd statement and couldn't have been further from the truth, since the national standards were in 100 percent conformity with the Policy Statement. All of the requirements within the national standards were carefully crafted by technical committee members from across the country through consensus agreement to ensure that they reflected the spirit of the Policy Statement and could be adopted in any jurisdiction and for any type of human research. As for funding private organizations, this precedent had already been set. The Canadian Association of Research Ethics Boards and the Canadian Council on Animal Care, both private sector organizations like ours, received annual funding from the three federal research funding agencies.

In light of our funding issues, we decided to rely on the expertise of our technical committee members to create the content of a comprehensive education program. It was a lot to ask, but members happily agreed to volunteer their time. Once the presentations were complete, we assembled a core group of members who would make presentations to stakeholders across the country.

OTHER HINTS THAT SOMETHING WAS AMISS

One of our initial presentations was with the office of the Secretariat. We met with the Secretariat's executive director in August of 2018, and during our meeting, guided her through the benefits of a Protection Program and its accreditation in creating a functional system of Canadian human research governance. We stressed that our initiative complemented the Secretariat's role in promoting responsible conduct of human research through its policies, like the Policy Statement, not only with eligible institutions, but with all organizations in Canada that conduct or oversee human research.

Our meeting yielded very few questions, but all things considered, we felt that the mood was positive, and at the end the executive director gave us kudos for our initiative.

A month later, feeling comfortable with the relationship we were nurturing with the Secretariat, we approached it with a request to add HRA Canada to a page on its website where it listed links to various stakeholder resources. A link to the American Accreditation Program was already there, so it was only logical to add a link to the Canadian accrediting body. The Secretariat replied to our request eight months later, in May 2019: "Thank you for your note. The webpage to which you refer is old and seldom visited, so it will be removed from our site within two weeks."

We later learned, again through an Access to Information and Privacy request, that our simple question had ignited a frenzy within the office of the Secretariat. The executive director did not want our accrediting body listed among its resources, so she demanded that this entire section of the website be deleted. Her rationale for this decision was redacted from the information request response we received.

Our next communication with the Secretariat was in May 2020. We wrote to the executive director and invited members of the Secretariat and its associated panel and committee members to participate with other stakeholders in the development of the national standards of Canada. Our request was declined without an explanation.

The tone of our email was inviting, inclusive, and representative of the type of outreach expected of an organization that develops national standards. At every opportunity during the development of the national standards, we invited stakeholders from all regions of the country and all facets of the human research landscape to participate, including the government. We strongly believed, as did other standards developers, that policy-makers were vital contributors to the development process. As a result, we continued to invite members of the Secretariat, its associated panels and committees, the federal research funding agencies, and the Health Canada Inspectorate to participate. We also notified them of when the national standards were published.

The Health Canada Inspectorate usually neglected to answer our email notifications. However, to one of our overtures it replied, "Thank you for your email inquiry, unfortunately Health Product Compliance (HPC) is responsible for compliance and enforcement activities related to health products." We interpreted this to mean that we should stay out of the Inspectorate's lane, as it alone was responsible for the oversight of drug trials in Canada. This was very unfortunate. We knew we needed to find a way to help the Inspectorate understand that there was a growing degree of non-compliance under its watch and it could benefit greatly from the national standards stakeholders were developing.

We were surprised to see that our communications with the three federal research funding agencies always ended up getting vetted by the Secretariat's executive director. In one email communication with the executive director, the president of the Social Sciences and Humanities Research Council expressed interest in the national standards, which included requirements not only for biomedical research, but also for research within the social sciences and humanities, the type of research that his council funded. In her reply, the executive director stated, in part, "Basically, [it's] a private initiative to create standards, and accredit institutions for developing human research protection programs that conform to those standards. They've been trying to recruit high-profile, credible people in the research community.... If you want to know more, let's arrange for a time to talk."

The executive director's choice of words indicated to us that something was amiss. Phrases like "high-profile, credible people" may have been chosen to indicate that we had no credibility on our own. By describing our initiative as "private," she may have been suggesting that national standards development and accreditation are activities of the public sector or government, which they are not.

The Secretariat's executive director wasted no time letting her opinions be known to her colleagues. Her views were recorded in the minutes of an internal meeting held in August 2020, where she prohibited her staff and members of panels and committees from participating in the development of the national standards, stating that this "may assume collaboration and endorsement."

Her efforts to influence the opinions of her colleagues proved to be successful and, in a few cases, interfered with the operations of our accrediting body. In one instance, as HRA Canada was about to embark on an accreditation assessment of an applicant, one of the site reviewers assigned to this assessment suddenly resigned. This site reviewer had just been appointed to the Interagency Advisory Panel on Research Ethics, which was associated with the Secretariat, and the Secretariat's executive director advised her that she must dissociate herself from our organization. The reason the site reviewer gave us for her resignation was that her mandate with us placed her in a situation of conflict of interest with her role on the panel. When we questioned her, she could not articulate what the particular conflict was, so we were not afforded an opportunity to manage it. Ironically, the two roles — that of a site reviewer with our organization and a member of the Interagency Advisory Panel on Research Ethics — were complementary. It seems that when our site reviewer had expressed an interest in becoming a panel member, her affiliation with our organization conflicted with the personal bias of the Secretariat's executive director. In our opinion, this was the conflict of interest she was referring to.

CANADIAN ASSOCIATION OF RESEARCH ETHICS BOARDS

The Canadian Association of Research Ethics Boards describes itself as a grassroots organization that represents the interests of all Canadian research ethics boards. The latter part of its self-portrayal is a bit of a stretch, since it has always excluded research ethics boards operating in the private sector. We found this confusing because, although it rejected my former company's research ethics board from its membership and meeting presentations, it regularly appealed to our board for sponsorship and funding of its annual meetings.

In 2018, the Canadian Association of Research Ethics Boards held its annual meeting in Montreal. The American Accreditation Program routinely presented at its annual meetings and was slated to make a presentation at this one. With our accreditation program newly functioning in Canada, it made sense for HRA Canada to share the stage. We were told that, because we were a "private" organization, we were not invited to participate in this meeting or any subsequent meetings. This excuse was ridiculous. The American Accreditation Program was a "private" organization. In fact, the Canadian Association of Research Ethics Boards only had to look at its own incorporation papers to see that it, too, was a "private" organization, incorporated as a Canadian non-profit organization in exactly the same way as our organizations.

In May 2021, shortly after we released the national standard on research ethics review to the public for consultation, a member of the Canadian Association of Research Ethics Boards' board of directors wrote a lengthy email to the Secretariat's executive director about HRA Canada and the Human Research Standards Organization, which he seemed to know very little about. He was concerned with "the interference of a private enterprise in the regulation of public research" (English translation from the original French quotation). He contemptuously alleged that both of our organizations were fraudulently incorporated and that their sole objective was to "privatize" oversight of all human research and profit from it.

This individual, in his position within the Canadian Association of Research Ethics Boards, must have known that his email, regardless of how foolish it made him look, would fall on friendly eyes and perhaps be shared. And that's exactly what happened. Fourteen minutes after receiving the email, the executive director forwarded it to everyone working within the Secretariat, to selected individuals within the associate panels and committees, and to the offices of the presidents of the three federal research funding agencies. Her email contained one word: "Interesting."

THE FIX WAS IN

One of the email recipients was a policy analyst at the Canadian Institutes of Health Research. That policy analyst sent an email to the executive director, stating, "I reviewed the HRSO [Human Research Standards Organization] standard for Ethical Review and Oversight of Human Research.... It is a very detailed operating standard that draws on the TCPS [the Policy Statement] and adds requirements from other standards. I couldn't find anything that goes against the TCPS requirements, but I'll admit that I dozed off a couple of times." Why this individual felt that she needed to add a comment about the national standard putting her to sleep points to her willingness to indulge the negative opinions of the executive director. As a policy analyst, this individual was very familiar with standards. She knew that the document she was reviewing was technical in nature and not some romance novel.

The minutes of a meeting held between the Secretariat and one of its panels in May 2021 recorded that the Secretariat would soon be announcing to the public that it was in no way affiliated with our organizations and that it did not support the national standards. This was terribly disappointing to read and underscored the

Secretariat's serious lack of understanding of the important role national standards played in setting requirements to meet policies, such as its Policy Statement.

The national standard, Ethical Review and Oversight of Human Research, mentioned in the policy analyst's email, was published in June 2021. It was a long time coming as it finally provided research ethics boards across the country with unambiguous and clear requirements for their conduct. Internal email communications revealed that the office of the Secretariat took issue with the fact that two members of one of its associated panels had participated in the standard's development. Of concern to the Secretariat was that their names were published on the list of technical committee members. The executive director closed the email thread with three words: "A bit disappointing."

According to emails exchanged between members of the Secretariat and panels in June 2021, they falsely concluded that we had purposely published the national standard on the very same day that the Secretariat published revisions to the Policy Statement, and that we did this to confuse the public. The executive director stated in the email thread that it "look[ed] planned and coordinated. Unfortunate."

As a standards development organization accredited by the Standards Council of Canada, the Human Research Standards Organization adhered strictly to the regulations and guidance requirements for national standards development. One of the requirements was that after a national standard had undergone a period of public consultation and the necessary modifications had been made to it, we had to submit it to the Standards Council of Canada, together with evidence to support its development, so that it could be considered for publication. Once it was in the hands of the standards council, we had no control whatsoever on the timing of its publication. It would have taken no time at all for the Secretariat to understand this publicly available process, yet it circulated a malicious conspiracy against us anyway.

A few weeks later, the executive director received an email from another member of the Canadian Association of Research Ethics Boards, who stated, "I recently became aware of the release of the Ethical Review and Oversight of Human Research standard.... While we have always supported the development of a national standard, we have some concerns with a 'for profit' organization coming forward and declaring their standard to be the national standard." Perhaps this individual was misinformed. The Secretariat's executive director was a lawyer and had a host of legal tools at her disposal to confirm that the Human Research Standards Organization was a legitimate non-profit standards development organization qualified and accredited by the Standards Council of Canada to develop national standards. She had an opportunity to shut down the misinformation in this person's email, but instead replied, "We are aware of this initiative. Happy to talk with you."

Unlike misinformation, which is the unintentional spreading of false or inaccurate information, disinformation is the intentional spreading of such information to mislead or influence others with the objective of causing harm. Was this the goal of the Secretariat's executive director?

We continued rolling out our presentations in the fall of 2021. A presentation scheduled with representatives of the University of Saskatchewan's research units was suddenly cancelled without explanation, and there was no further discussion to reschedule it. We later learned that the director of the research ethics office at the University of Saskatchewan — who was the former vice-president of the Canadian Association of Research Ethics Boards and had close ties to the Secretariat's executive director — requested that our presentation be cancelled. In her email to the vice-dean of research at the University of Saskatchewan, she made a series of misleading and defamatory statements about the national standard, implying that it was not a legitimate national standard of Canada. She falsely claimed that our standard conflicted with the Policy Statement.

A few months later we requested to present to the research ethics board at the University of Western Ontario. We received a reply within minutes. However, as we read it, it was evident that we had been copied on the email reply by mistake. The email had been written by the university's director of research ethics and compliance. In addition to numerous factual errors, this individual made the following false statement: "Currently Canada does not have a national accreditation in place and there is no federal endorsement for this type of accreditation at this time…. I do not think this NSC [national standard of Canada] is something we need to consider at this time."

We responded to this individual, copying all of the email's recipients, and corrected her false and misleading information. I received a curt email response apologizing for mistakenly copying me on her email, but not for anything else.

Shortly thereafter, at the end of a virtual presentation to more than fifty research ethics board colleagues affiliated with Michael Smith Health Research British Columbia, we opened the floor for questions. Up to this point, the presentation had gone smoothly and the meeting participants had seemed very interested and engaged with the content. One of the first questions came from the University of British Columbia's director of research ethics. She angrily stated that she had so many questions, she didn't know where to start. She proceeded to monopolize the entire question period with a bitter diatribe against accreditation and standards. She incorporated inaccurate and false descriptions of our organizations in her argument, such as labelling them as for-profit and mocking us for not having secured any public funding or support. Her tone was mean-spirited and demeaning, and even though I had never met her before, she didn't hesitate to launch an attack on me personally. The meeting moderators tried to cut her off numerous times, but she managed to demand centre stage for almost thirty minutes in a cringeworthy rant.

This individual was a lawyer, and like the Secretariat's executive director, was fully aware of the importance of factual information and the consequences of defamation. She was also a past president of the Canadian Association of Research Ethics Boards, which gave us insight into where her alternate facts were coming from.

In an email to her colleagues after our presentation she wrote, "They have recruited a number of credible mostly academic individuals like Michael McDonald to be on their various advisory boards.... [T]he Secretariat is somewhat sceptical.... The bottom line from what I can see, is that they want to make this a profitable initiative.... Personally, I think that they want to privatize the whole ethics review/monitoring process.... I would be happy to chat with you further, but don't want to put anything more than the above in an e-mail." Whether she was aware that her accusations were baseless and false is unknown.

Disinformation is difficult to combat because the underlying reasons for the malice are usually subjective. The disparaging comments made by some of the people presented in this chapter were based on misinformation, which when disseminated, cast doubt on our initiative and had the potential to cause irreparable harm. To counter and contain the misinformation and assuage stakeholders' concerns, we presented the following facts.

First and foremost, our initiative, a human research accreditation program rooted in the national standards of Canada, was conceived many years ago by two independent groups with the support and funding of the federal government. Their published reports addressed the enormous gaps in human research governance and created a safer environment for research participants. Alongside hundreds of volunteer stakeholders and without any public funding, we materialized the concept.

The Human Research Standards Organization is incorporated as an independent, non-profit entity in Canada. It was accredited by the Standards Council of Canada, which granted it the unique ability to develop, maintain, and publish national standards of Canada. The company does not sell anything, so it does not generate revenues. Like many standards development organizations, it releases its national standards to the public free of charge.

HRA Canada is also an independent, non-profit organization. Its accreditation program is supported by the national standards of Canada published by the Human Research Standards Organization, and it mimics the corporate structure and operations of Accreditation Canada and the Canadian Council on Animal Care.

The funds derived from HRA Canada's accreditation services are revenues, not profits. These revenues cover operating costs, including compensation of site reviewers, accreditation council members, and advisory board members for their time. No revenues have ever been paid to me in salary or other compensation.

Each year, the company has operated at a loss, and personal funds have had to be infused to cover the shortfalls. This is not uncommon for a start-up non-profit organization. As the company accredits more Protection Programs, this imbalance will be somewhat resolved. (As you may recall, the Canadian Council on Animal Care's operating expenses are compensated by the federal research funding agencies.)

For the most part, my role as creator of the initiative is done, and I play a minor role in the administration of the organizations. Canadian stakeholders in human research, including research participants, drive the need for new standards to be developed. It is the responsibility of technical committee members, the majority of whom work in public institutions, to develop the standards. Regarding the accreditation of Protection Programs, the objective assessments of their conformity and compliance are the work of site reviewers. Determination of accreditation status is accomplished by members of the accreditation council. More than half of HRA Canada's site reviewers and accreditation council members currently work in public institutions or are retired from their careers in such institutions.

Like any stakeholder, the government can participate in national standards development. It can also make accreditation mandatory through legislation or policy. However, it cannot control these processes because of its susceptibility to political pressures and interference, which have the potential to threaten the impartiality necessary for objective oversight. The Canadian Council on Animal Care, Accreditation Canada, and the American Accreditation Program are all independent (non-government), non-profit organizations that rely on the standards developed within their organization or by their partner organizations for their programs. HRA Canada operates no differently from these organizations in the accreditation of human research.

WHAT WAS THE SECRETARIAT'S ENDGAME?

As listed in the Terms of Reference section on its web page, one of the responsibilities of the Secretariat with respect to its associated panels and the three federal research funding agencies is to manage allegations of policy breaches and to ensure that the eligible institution where an alleged policy breach occurred conducts its own investigation "properly."[2] However, when it was challenged to abide by its mandate, the Secretariat caved. Formal complaints of numerous and serious alleged policy breaches were filed with the Secretariat in 2024 for both the Prince Albert School Study and the Montreal pediatric oncology study. The Secretariat shocked the Canadian research community when it defended its inaction by announcing that, despite what is written in the policies, its mandate regarding policy breaches was limited to studies that were funded by the federal government. (Recall that the Prince Albert School Study had been funded by Pure North S'Energy Foundation, and the Montreal pediatric oncology study had been funded by the hospital.) This rendered the Secretariat's entire scope of oversight to a small minority of Canadian studies. If this was the policy of the Secretariat all along, it was certainly not the understanding of our colleagues across the country.

Nowhere in its mandate is the Secretariat given power to thwart the activities of a non-government organization in its efforts to create a functional system of objective oversight and accountability for human research. Nowhere in its mandate does it have the authority to manufacture mistruths about a non-government organization and abuse its position of influence to stifle the adoption of a much-needed human research accreditation program.

What is ironic is that another of the responsibilities of the Secretariat, as listed on its web page, is to "participate in the ongoing national discussion regarding the development of an oversight system for research ethics review practices." It certainly failed this part of its mandate. In fact, it made certain that no discussions concerning oversight would even occur.

The Secretariat has never attempted to explain its malicious actions against us. Some colleagues have opined that it may feel threatened by our initiative and that its role in the research ethics enterprise may be diminished by our presence. The Secretariat wants us to believe that it plays an active role in research participant protection and the oversight of ethical human research. National standards and accreditation complicate the Secretariat's messaging and raise important questions concerning the gaps in oversight, accountability, and transparency.

Perhaps the Secretariat doesn't have an endgame. It may not even know why it continues, as it has for almost twenty years, to resist changes to the status quo despite the numerous tragic reminders that the current human research system is unsustainable without proper governance.

MASLOW'S HAMMER

American psychologist Abraham Maslow wrote in 1966, "It is tempting, if the only tool you have is a hammer, to treat everything as if it were a nail."[3] This phrase became known as Maslow's hammer or the law of the instrument. It refers to the cognitive bias we apply to situations and issues when we rely on what is familiar to us. In many situations, Maslow's hammer can lead to tunnel vision, preventing us from seeking new solutions to problems and inhibiting the process of change.

If we evaluate potential solutions to the problems we face based solely on the skills we have, we become unable to seek or consider alternative solutions that may be more suitable and efficient. The skills of many of the individuals presented in this chapter hinged on the functioning of research ethics boards. Through this lens, they couldn't fully appreciate the significance of the development of a Protection Program and the value of its accreditation. The fact that accreditation is a quality assurance program was not a concept they seemed to appreciate.

Over the last two decades, millions of dollars have flowed from federal and provincial research funding agencies into projects aimed at increasing efficiencies in the research ethics review process. Even if these projects were successful, which we have not seen any evidence of to date, they would only have the potential to make minor changes to the issues associated with the governance of human research in our country. Like rearranging the deck chairs on the *Titanic*, creating the most efficient ethics review process is useful only if the ship is intact. The proper way to make ethics review efficient would be to include it as a component of an accredited Protection Program.

A NEW SHIP'S CAPTAIN?

In September 2022, the Secretariat's executive director took a medical leave of absence from her job and sadly passed away four months later. The appointment of her interim and then permanent replacement was announced shortly thereafter. Curious to know if the new executive director had a different perspective on national standards and accreditation from that of her predecessor, we met with her and her staff in September 2023. By all accounts, the Secretariat now appeared genuinely interested in our initiative. The meeting ended with an air of cautious optimism that we could move forward together, if not in parallel.

We continued under this assumption until we learned from an Access to Information and Privacy request that, less than thirty minutes after our meeting, members of the Secretariat exchanged internal emails criticizing our work and our people. Meeting with us had been nothing more than a ruse.

In February 2024, we sent a letter to the presidents of the three federal research funding agencies, as well as to all of the other stakeholders in human research in Canada who had formed the Sponsors'. Table that issued the Experts Committee's *Moving Ahead* report back in 2008. The *Moving Ahead* report, like the National Council's Accreditation Proposal that came before it, provided Canadians with a blueprint for a good and ethical governance system and was a foundational document in the creation of the Human Research Standards Organization and HRA Canada. Because it was not a member of the Sponsors' Table, the Secretariat was not a recipient of our letter.

Our letter outlined the problems with the current system of human research governance and argued for the adoption of a program of oversight and accountability through the accreditation of Protection Programs. It also drew comparisons between the system of governance we were proposing and the one operated by the

Canadian Council on Animal Care, noting that in our country, animals seem to be better protected in research than humans.

We asked that the three federal research funding agencies support the accreditation of Canadian Protection Programs by providing HRA Canada with operating funds consistent with the funding model of the Canadian Council on Animal Care. And using the Montreal pediatric oncology study to exemplify how the agencies seem to be funding researchers without any guardrails, we requested that Protection Program accreditation become a condition of funding, similar to how the granting of funds for animal research is conditional upon certification from the Canadian Council on Animal Care.

We ended our letter with the Privy Council's landmark decision the prior year that its potential vendors of human research services must exist within a Protection Program and be in good accreditation standing with either HRA Canada or the American Accreditation Program. We stressed that by placing this condition on potential vendors, the Privy Council was publicly acknowledging that the assurance it required in choosing potential vendors could not be satisfied through the current system of governance, and that Protection Program accreditation gave it the assurance it needed.

Of the thirty-three recipients of our letter, only three replied. The first reply came from the president of the University of Toronto, who summed up his thoughts in two lines: "Thank you ... for your message and for sharing your thoughts and concerns on this matter. However, we respectfully decline to participate in this initiative."

The second came from Alberta's minister of health. Her response was lengthy, and we were impressed that she took the time to investigate the matter. Unfortunately, it echoed the same rhetoric we had been hearing for years and was replete with false assumptions. For example, she wrote that "policy requirements, oversight by funding agencies, and the supportive role of PRE [the Interagency Advisory Panel on Research Ethics] ensure that research involving human participants is conducted ethically." She continued, "Compliance with the TCPS [the Policy Statement] is mandatory and a condition of funding from any of the three federal agencies; failure to fulfill the requirements of the TCPS may result in recourse by the agencies."

We received the third response in mid-June 2024. It was sent to us by the new executive director of the Secretariat, who was writing, as she alleged, on behalf of the three federal research funding agencies. The letter lacked substance and failed to address any of the issues we had presented. Suspicious of this response, we filed an Access to Information and Privacy request. We learned that we were not wrong to infer that the letter came solely from the Secretariat, and not from the federal research funding agencies. In an email to the federal research funding agencies, the Secretariat's executive director wrote, "The Secretariat has learned that all three Agencies have received the attached letter … as they were members of the Sponsors Table referred to at the outset of the letter. The Secretariat is familiar with the work of Human Research Accreditation Canada and has had previous communications with them…. According to the Secretariat, the request is not urgent because the subject of 'Human Research Accreditation' has been the subject of much discussion for many years."

The Secretariat then proposed that it prepare a response to our letter on behalf of the federal research funding agencies, as it considered that our letter did not require anything more than to be treated "secretarially." We were very disappointed when we couldn't find any evidence to indicate that the offices of the presidents of the federal research funding agencies had even read our letter.

Once again, the Secretariat proved that they would never be part of the solution. We decided to take our case to another level of government, outside the narrow focus of the bureaucrats we had been appealing to for years. On July 20, 2024, we launched a House of Commons petition to request that the government equalize protections for humans in research to those that had been in place for animals for almost forty years. Under the Tri-Agency Agreement on the Administration of Agency Grants and Awards by Research Institutions, "if the Institution uses animals in any of its research, whether in its own facilities, in other facilities or in the field, it shall ... maintain a valid Certificate of Good Animal Practice from the Canadian Council on Animal Care ('CCAC') and ensure that research funded by an Agency complies fully with CCAC standards."[4]

Our demand was simple: What has been recognized for years as good and ethical governance of animal research must also apply to research involving humans. In no way were we asking the government to hold research funding in abeyance. We were asking it to think of the future of human research before it spent our hard-earned tax dollars. A better tomorrow would require the government to invest funds to improve the infrastructure of eligible institutions, including the development of their Protection Programs and procedures for eventual accreditation.

Our petition received the requisite number of signatures and was certified by the government. At the time of this writing, it has not yet been presented to the House of Commons for consideration. In the meantime, our proposal for a functional governance framework for human research is reaching the ears of the decision-makers in the Canadian government. Our argument that there is no logical reason for animals to be better protected in research than humans seems to be resonating. Our fight is not over yet. Stay tuned.

CONCLUSION

THE OPPORTUNITY TO PARTICIPATE IN A RESEARCH STUDY MAY PRESENT ITSELF at any point in your life. You may decide to participate simply because you are curious about the research topic or process or because you wish to help your community. For your participation you may receive a small incentive or reward, but for the most part, your decision to participate would be an unencumbered one.

If you suffer from an illness or disease, a research study may open the door to a potential therapeutic treatment or cure. Or you may seek research participation as a solution to an acute financial problem. In both of these scenarios, your decision to participate in human research may be confounded by external factors.

A friend of mine, whom I will refer to as Liam to protect his privacy, was diagnosed with young-onset Parkinson's disease. It progressed slowly, and for a few years he was able to do most of the things he enjoyed, like skiing. On winter weekends, our two families would get together, and if Liam was feeling well enough, he would usher us down the most challenging runs.

Liam had told his doctor that he wanted to be considered for any clinical trials for which he met the eligibility criteria. He had two university degrees and was a very intelligent and witty man, yet he could seldom produce detailed information on the particular study he was participating in at any given time. Liam was desperate for an effective treatment or cure for his disease, and as the years went by, he seemed to adopt a cavalier attitude toward study participation. He seemed uninterested in the study medication he was taking, its potential side effects, or the potential dangers of participating in consecutive clinical trials without a proper washout period.

In some respects, I became an advocate for Liam as he navigated through the mire of clinical trials presented to him for consideration. These trials were carried out under the auspices of a major Canadian university teaching hospital, and Liam's doctor doubled as the study investigator for most of them. I was stunned by the countless deficiencies and errors I found in the information that was supplied to Liam, including the informed consent forms. It was hard to believe that study information of such poor quality had been approved by the research ethics board of a prestigious Canadian institution.

The parents of the children in the Montreal pediatric oncology study experienced an incalculable and unimaginable degree of desperation. Their children suffered from cancers that had not been helped by previous treatment attempts. These parents agreed to place their children in the oncology trial in an ultimate attempt to save their children's lives. The parents were lured by the promise that the study would induce remission. However, disease remission was one of the experimental outcomes of the trial — in other words, whether it could be achieved was unknown and under investigation. Despite this, the researchers did the unthinkable: They told the parents that their children would achieve remission in the study.

Similarly, the parents of the Indigenous children who participated in the Prince Albert School Study agreed to enrol their children in an effort to break the cycle of intergenerational trauma that had afflicted their communities for over one hundred years. The parents were lured by the promise that the study would improve their children's performance at school and the quality of their relationships and would reduce the fear and anxiety associated with the trauma that had been passed down to them. The researchers had no evidence that the study would benefit the children, and it was unethical for them to make such claims to the parents.

The financial problems that plagued Leticia, Henri, Baptiste, and Mohsen placed them in a state of desperation. They were lured into study participation by the promise of large sums of money. Early-phase researchers used various types of study advertisements that aggrandized the monetary compensation, and they strategically placed these advertisements where those in situations of financial vulnerability would notice them.

Someone in a state of desperation may find themselves overwhelmed with feelings of hopelessness, despair, and anxiety. They may focus their energy on finding ways to get out of the situation they are in and make impulsive choices that may not be in their best interest, like agreeing to participate in a research study.

Once attracted or lured, potential research participants commit to participating in the study when they sign the informed consent form. Their signature confirms that they have understood all the information provided to them and were given ample time to make a free and informed decision. If the study includes an intervention, like a drug, they agree that they have understood the risks associated with taking it, as well as all other risks associated with their participation.

Most researchers and research ethics boards are not equipped to assess the complex mindset of an individual who sees a research study as a desperate attempt to solve a situational problem. "They signed the informed consent form, so they knew the risks" is something we often hear from the research team when things go wrong. Recall that SFBC Anapharm blamed the tuberculosis outbreak on Baptiste, a research participant from Haiti. Like others participating in the study, Baptiste was, as a fellow research participant noted, "blinded by the money, [and] ... completely missed the detail."[1] When a person's vulnerabilities are targeted for the purpose of enticing them to participate in research, their consent is not provided freely and their level of understanding of the study information is questionable at best.

Even though informed consent forms include wording about a research participant's right to leave the study at any time and for any reason, we have seen how difficult this can be to accomplish in practice. Leticia and some of the research participants in the Prince Albert School Study faced monetary and physical barriers to withdrawing that forced them to continue participating in their studies against their own better judgment.

To minimize harms, an individual's unique life situation must be studied before they can be considered for participation in a research study. Their mental, social, spiritual, and emotional state must be evaluated alongside the physical to determine if there are any complicating factors influencing their decision to participate in research.

Liam was intent on trying to determine which treatment arm of a study he was assigned to. I recall one time when he spilled the contents of his study capsules onto a plate and added drops of different solvents to the white powdery pile to test his theory that he had been assigned to the placebo group. If he could prove his theory correct, he would be less inclined to comply with the study procedures, in the hopes that he would be withdrawn and considered for a new study. In a similar vein, both Henri and Baptiste withheld vital medical information from the research staff so that they could meet the study entry criteria. Liam, Henri, and Baptiste lacked an understanding of how important they were to the research process and how critical their compliance was to the integrity of the study and the quality of the data. The research system failed them.

Acknowledging that the current system of human research governance is broken is the first step in adopting a solution to fix it. Until then, the protection of research participants' rights, safety, and welfare will remain an illusion. Without a program of objective oversight and accountability, and real consequences for bad actors, it is incumbent on anyone contemplating research participation to fully and completely understand their rights and to demand that those rights be upheld and protected. This is a lot to ask of someone who is already struggling.

———————

Issues of non-compliance in human research are entertained by Health Canada, the Secretariat on Responsible Conduct of Research, and the media. All employ after-the-fact approaches, and only the media makes it its mission to disseminate the information it gathers to the public. As presented in this book, the media was often the first source of information regarding tragedies in human research, leaving the government feverishly playing catch-up on the details. This is not a system that is feasible, transparent, or sustainable.

Health Canada and the Secretariat respond to complaints in different ways. Some of the tragedies explored in this book, like Henri's death, the tuberculosis outbreak, and the Montreal pediatric oncology study, revealed that Health Canada did conduct inspections after the harms had occurred. As Health Canada stated in recent interviews, issues of research ethics "fall under the purview of REBs [research ethics boards]."[2] It is, therefore, not surprising that the Health Canada inspections failed to detect violations of research participants' rights despite the fact they were in plain sight and were the causes of the harms inflicted.

Health Canada shifted the responsibility for overseeing research ethics issues onto research ethics boards without ensuring, through proper oversight, that these boards operated according to the same rigorous standards across the country. The conduct exhibited by the University of Regina research ethics board in its review of the Prince Albert School Study is an egregious example of why a system of objective oversight is mandatory for proper governance.

This also raises concerns about the drugs approved for sale in Canada. How does Health Canada ensure that the data it reviews in determining its drug approvals were derived from human research that was conducted ethically and responsibly? Perhaps this is a topic for another book.

Health Canada can easily remedy these chasms of oversight by making Protection Program accreditation a condition for authorizing clinical trials. This condition would apply both to the investigative site(s) and to the research ethics board(s) presented in the application for clinical trial authorization. Then, and only then, can Health Canada claim that it contributes to safeguarding the rights, safety, and welfare of research participants. This proactive measure may prevent harms from occurring in the first place.

How the Secretariat responds to complaints is not straightforward. It seems that it has a mandate to investigate breaches of the federal research funding agencies' policies. However, the Secretariat did not investigate the complaints regarding the Prince Albert School Study and the Montreal pediatric oncology study, despite the numerous policy breaches committed by the institutions involved. It said it only considers action for research funded by the federal government. In an interview with Geoff Leo, Martin

Letendre pondered, "Why does the Secretariat even exist? What's the point if you're only looking at a tiny percentage [of studies]?"[3]

Canada needs a functional system of objective oversight to protect research participants' rights, safety, and welfare throughout the entire life cycle of their research participation, regardless of the type of research they are participating in or the research's funding source.

———————

A good and ethical human research governance system needs to include a robust system of accountability for serious breaches. At a minimum, it should remove public research funding from culpable researchers and prevent refunding without specific, objective assurance criteria. Taxpayers need to know that their hard-earned money is not being used to support researchers who cause them harm, or harm their families, neighbours, or friends.

Animal research governance in Canada is good and ethical. An independent organization, the Canadian Council on Animal Care — a non-profit entity established in exactly the same way as our organizations were — developed research-based standards and a complementary program of oversight to ensure that those conducting animal research are conforming to those standards. Two of Canada's three research funding agencies invest millions of taxpayer dollars annually to ensure the viability of the Canadian Council on Animal Care because they rely on the assurance that the council's objective assessments provide. Yet, because of the limited perspective bias of some influential bureaucrats, a parallel system of objective oversight for human research has been sidelined for the last twenty years. As Catherine Schuppli and Dr. Michael McDonald wrote in 2005, "The existing governance system for research animals offers important insights and experiences that seem directly relevant to the improvement of Canadian governance of human research protection.... [T]he absence of a system of accreditation for Canadian human research protection and the lack of information about the system as a whole makes it impossible to reassure Canadians that they are adequately protected as research subjects."[4]

Year after year, Canada's three federal research funding agencies award funds to researchers without any assurance that the rights, safety, and welfare of human research participants will be protected. I hope I have demonstrated that there is a better way for us to move forward together.

———

Canadians must have agency to make informed decisions about research participation, and they must have confidence that their rights, safety, and welfare will be protected at every stage of the research life cycle. These are the hallmarks of a Protection Program, which, once accredited, ensures that these safeguards are supported and practised.

For governance to be good and ethical, it needs to apply to all human research and address the obvious gaps in oversight, accountability, and transparency. Protection Program accreditation is an objective assessment of quality that can be implemented by the government to address these gaps. As a conditional element in clinical trial authorization and human research funding, the government can adopt Protection Program accreditation to prevent future harms to research participants. It will take a strong collective desire to overcome the urge to resist change and adopt the elements necessary to make human research safer for Canadians.

ACKNOWLEDGEMENTS

I USED TO THINK THAT WRITING A BOOK WAS A LONELY, GRUELLING ENDEAVOUR — but I couldn't have been more wrong. Writing does require discipline (consistent effort) and a lifetime of preparation (reading), but in many ways, it is a team sport. I want to thank the many members of my team for helping make this book a reality.

To my daughter, Halie Mei Jensen, thank you for your insightful and thoughtful analysis of the many issues raised in this book. Your gentle and perceptive critiques made all the difference. Thank you for helping me to see this book through your brilliant brown eyes. I love you.

When I began writing this book, I brought together a circle of reviewers. Each member brought their unique superpower to the group. Joanne Moss, thank you for your boundless empathy — you helped me transform ideas and words into feelings. Colleen Cochran, thank you for asking all the good questions. No, it's not just you — we all agree that your questions need to be addressed; you're just brave enough to ask them. Emile Girard, my neighbour and friend, thank you for sharing a love of books, our forest and lake, and the natural world around us. Your perspective is your superpower, for which I am so grateful. Alex Karabanow, I am deeply grateful for your extensive knowledge of research ethics in our country and for your unwavering loyalty to our cause. Your guidance was invaluable, and so much of this could not have been accomplished without you.

To Clarissa — you are my daily source of sanity, laughter, and encouragement. Your sharp eye for detail, incredible intelligence, and boundless kindness made this journey not only possible but also enjoyable. You spent countless hours with me, almost daily, helping shape this book, and your steady presence and tireless help brought it to life. Thank you for your unwavering support, your cheerful spirit, and for always being in my corner.

I would also like to extend my deepest gratitude to Martin Letendre. As a lawyer and research ethicist — one of very few in Canada — you are an unmatched source of expertise. But beyond that, you are my friend, a brother from another mother. In over twenty years of knowing you, I have never heard you speak a foul word about anyone, a testament to your kindness and integrity. I feel so lucky to have you in my life, and I am especially grateful for the time and care you put into reviewing this book. Your wisdom and friendship mean the world to me.

To Dr. Michael McDonald, my deepest gratitude for penning the foreword to this book. For years, you have been a guiding force in research ethics, illuminating both its principles and real-world applications. Your extensive body of work has reinforced our shared responsibility to protect the rights, safety, and well-being of research participants at every stage. Your contribution to this book — and to the field as a whole — is invaluable. Thank you for your generosity, insight, and unyielding commitment.

Heartfelt thanks to Pierre Deschamps, whose pioneering work laid the foundation for research ethics in Canada. In 1995, you shaped the way we think about formally protecting humans in research, and your influence continues to guide us today. Your dedication, both through your scholarship and your ongoing role on our advisory board, has been instrumental. Thank you for your leadership, vision, and steadfast commitment to this cause.

I am also deeply grateful to the other members of our advisory board — Michael McDonald, Michael Owen, and Eric Meslin — who, alongside Pierre, provide invaluable support and sage advice. Your collective wisdom has strengthened our work in immeasurable ways.

To Henri's siblings — Arthur, Leo, Odile, and Thérèse — thank you for the hours you spent with me, helping me truly know and understand Henri, your beloved brother. Through your stories, I came to see his life in full: from birth to death, his marriages, his children, and the boundless generosity that defined him. Even in his final moments, his selflessness never wavered. A special thanks to Arthur — your humour brought light to even the heaviest conversations, and together, we cried, remembered, and honoured Henri's life.

To the investigative journalists whose courage brought the many research tragedies to light, thank you. Your relentless pursuit of truth ensured that these stories were told from the perspective of those who were harmed, reminding us all that research participants are human beings, not just statistics. A special shout-out to Geoff Leo, David Evans, Michael Smith, Liz Willen, Pasquale Turbide, Normand Grondin, Martin Patriquin, Jean Heller, Max Binks-Collier, Masih Khalatbari, Charlie Buckley, Robert Cribb, and all those I may have unintentionally left out — your work has made a lasting impact.

A deep thank you to my literary agent, Tim Brandhorst. From the very beginning, you have been a bold champion of this book. Your vision and determination transformed my concept into something beyond what I could have imagined: a book any publisher would be eager to publish. Your insight, guidance, and belief in this project made all the difference. I am deeply grateful.

A sincere thank you to my editor, Russell Smith, from Dundurn Press. Your keen eye, high standards, and honest feedback pushed me to strengthen this book in ways I couldn't have done alone. I am deeply grateful for your expertise and your commitment to excellence, and for challenging me to make this book the best it could be.

A heartfelt thank you to Laura Boyle and Karen Alexiou at Dundurn Press for the stunning cover design of this book. You captured its essence beautifully, translating the book's message into a visual that is both striking and deeply meaningful. I am truly grateful for your creativity and talent.

I am deeply grateful to Susan Fitzgerald, my magnificent copy editor, whose sharp eye, thoughtful edits, and deep respect for the text elevated this manuscript in every way. And a heartfelt note of thanks to the other wonderful members of the editorial team at Dundurn Press — especially Elena Radic and Janna Green — for their patience, support, and guidance.

I would also like to thank Meghan Macdonald, my publisher, for her support of this manuscript and for helping to make its publication possible. And to Eden Boudreau, my publicist, thank you for your energy and enthusiasm in preparing this book for the world's eyes. I've learned so much from everyone at Dundurn Press. Thank you.

And lastly, to Olivia, my ever-patient canine companion. Month after month, you stayed by my side as I poured long hours into writing — sometimes at the cost of your beloved forest walks and kayak rides. Your quiet understanding, unwavering presence, and gentle nudges reminding me to take a break meant more to me than you'll ever know.

NOTES

FOREWORD

1   Susan M. Cox et al., "Epistemic Strategies in Ethical Review: REB Members' Experiences of Assessing Probable Impacts of Research for Research Subjects," *Journal of Empirical Research on Human Research Ethics* 15, no. 5 (2019): 1–13, doi.org/10.1177/1556264619872369.

2   James A. Anderson et al., "Research Ethics, Broadly Writ: Beyond REB Review," *Health Law Review* 19, no. 3 (2011): 12–24.

3   Daryl Pullman, "Research Governance, Bio-Politics, and Political Will: Recent Lessons from Newfoundland and Labrador," *Health Law Review* 13, no. 2/3 (2005): 75–79. In 2006, the province passed the Health Research Ethics Authority Act to require oversight of health research. I chaired the three-person committee advising the Government of Newfoundland and Labrador; see Michael McDonald et al., *External Consultants' Report on Proposed Health Research Ethics Board for Newfoundland and Labrador* (August 2001).

4   Michael McDonald and Eric Meslin, "Research Ethics as Social Policy: Some Lessons from Experiences in Canada and the United States," *Tocqueville Review/La Revue Tocqueville* 24, no. 2 (2003): 61–85.

INTRODUCTION

1   Laura Eggertson, "Lancet Retracts 12-Year-Old Article Linking Autism to MMR Vaccines," *CMAJ* 182, no. 4 (2010): E199–E200.

2   T.S. Sathyanarayana Rao and Chittaranjan Andrade, "The MMR Vaccine and Autism: Sensation, Refutation, Retraction, and Fraud," *Indian Journal of Psychiatry* 53, no. 2 (2011): 95–96.

3   David B. Resnik, "What Is Ethics in Research and Why Is It Important?," National Institute of Environmental Health Sciences, last updated December 23, 2024, niehs.nih.gov/research /resources/bioethics/whatis.

I: A SUSPICIOUS DEATH

1   Matej Mikulic, "Generics Share of Medicine Prescriptions in Canada from 2006 to 2023," Statista, June 3, 2024, statista.com/statistics /473165/generic-precription-market-share-in-canada.

2   This is true for most drugs that are given orally. To demonstrate bioequivalence for drugs that are administered in other ways, such as topically, parenterally, or through inhalation, comparative clinical trial testing is required in addition to these pharmacokinetic studies. Additionally, Health Canada has different bioequivalence criteria for drugs that have a narrow therapeutic range or are highly toxic, such as digoxin, lithium, and warfarin.

3   Shein-Chung Chow, "Bioavailability and Bioequivalence in Drug Development," *WIREs Computational Statistics* 6, no. 4 (2014): 304–12, doi.org/10.1002/wics.1310.

2: "WHERE DID YOU GET THAT CANOE?"

1   "SFBC Acquires Anapharm," *Lexpert*, March 18, 2002, lexpert.ca /big-deals/sfbc-acquires-anapharm/343265.

2   C. Haney et al., "Interpersonal Dynamics in a Simulated Prison," *International Journal of Criminology and Penology* 1, no. 1 (1973): 69–97.

3   "Health and Well-Being," World Health Organization, accessed February 18, 2025, who.int/data/gho/data/major-themes/health -and-well-being.

4   "Healthy Living," Health Canada, last modified November 30, 2023, canada.ca/en/health-canada/services/healthy-living.html.

5   P. Fortun et al., "Recall of Informed Consent Information by Healthy Volunteers in Clinical Trials," *QJM* 101, no. 8 (2008): 625–29, doi.org/10.1093/qjmed/hcn067.

4: "WHAT'S A FEW GRAND TO PROTECT YOUR REPUTATION?"

1   David Evans, "SFBC Drug Testers Have Tuberculosis After Exposure," *Bloomberg News,* December 15, 2005, quoted in Vera Hassner Sharav, "Montreal Clinical Trial Subjects Exposed to Tuberculosis," Alliance for Human Research Protection, December 15, 2005, ahrp.org /montreal-clinical-trial-subjects-expoxed-to-tuberculosis.

2   "Cobayes humains," Enquête, Radio-Canada, November 7, 2008.

3   Martin Patriquin, "Inside the Human Guinea Pig Capital of North America," *Maclean's,* August 25, 2009, macleans.ca/society/health /inside-the-human-guinea-pig-capital-of-north-america.

5: THE CONSEQUENCES OF NO CONSEQUENCES

1   "About Inspections of Clinical Trials for Human Drugs," Government of Canada, last modified December 9, 2015, canada.ca/en/health-canada /services/inspecting-monitoring-drug-health-products/drug-health -product-inspections/about-inspections-clinical-trials-human-drugs .html.

2   "Clinical Trial Application — Amendments (CTA-As)," Health Canada, last modified September 9, 2014, canada.ca/en/health-canada /services/drugs-health-products/drug-products/applications -submissions/guidance-documents/clinical-trials/application -amendments.html.

3   Michael Goodyear, "Learning from the TGN1412 Trial," editorial, *BMJ* (March 22, 2006), doi.org/10.1136/bmj.38797.635012.47.

4   "Requirements for Tuberculosis Screening of Healthy Volunteers in Phase I Clinical Trials Involving Immunosuppressant Drugs or Drugs with Immunosuppressant Properties," Health Canada, July 23, 2006, canada.ca/en/health-canada/services/drugs-health-products /drug-products/applications-submissions/guidance-documents

/clinical-trials/notice-clinical-trial-sponsors-requirements-tuberculosis
-screening-healthy-volunteers-phase-clinical-trials-involving
-immunosuppressant-drugs.html; Canadian Press, "Health Canada
Introduces Trial Rules in Wake of Tuberculosis Scare," *CBC News*,
October 16, 2006, cbc.ca/news/science/health-canada-introduces-
trial-rules-in-wake-of-tuberculosis-scare-1.602677.

5   Kirsty Barnes, "Troubled SFBC Changes Its Name in Hope of
Changing Its Fortunes," Outsourcing Pharma, August 30, 2006.

6: GAPS IN OVERSIGHT

1   Joel Lexchin, "Health Canada and Big Pharma: Too Close for
Comfort," *The Conversation*, August 12, 2019, theconversation.com
/health-canada-and-big-pharma-too-close-for-comfort-120965.

2   Martin Letendre and Sébastien Lanctôt, "Le cadre juridique régissant
la relation entre le chercheur et le sujet de recherche: la sécurité conférée
par le droit canadien et le droit québécois est-elle illusoire?," *Les Cahiers
de droit* 48, no. 4 (2007): 579–633, doi.org.10.7202/043947ar.

3   Health Products and Food Branch Inspectorate, *Summary
Report of Inspections of Clinical Trials Conducted from April 2004
to March 2011* (Health Canada, 2012), canada.ca/en/health
-canada/services/drugs-health-products/compliance-enforcement
/good-clinical-practices/reports/summary-report-inspections
-clinical-trials-conducted-april-2004-march-2011.html.

4   There is a workaround to this problem: If a specific clinical trial is
publicly registered on ClinicalTrials.gov in the United States (all
trials should be registered, but many are not), and if it received
funding from the Canadian Institutes of Health Research, one
can identify the investigator by triangulating information from
the Inspectorate's clinical trial database, the ClinicalTrials
.gov registry, and the Canadian Institutes of Health Research's
funding database.

5   Jesse McLean and David Bruser, "Drug-Testing Rules Broken by
Canadian Researchers," *Toronto Star*, September 16, 2014, thestar
.com/news/canada/drug-testing-rules-broken-by-canadian-researchers
/article_93e17de1-6f2f-5f70-9ef7-6ea1f167f6d7.html.

6 Robert Cribb et al., "Inside Canada's 'Exploitative' Clinical Trial Industry, Where Study Participants Say They're Incentivized to Lie — Even About Medications' Side Effects," *Toronto Star*, September 25, 2024, posted October 7, 2024, at Investigative Journalism Bureau, University of Toronto, ijb.utoronto.ca/news/inside-canadas -exploitative-clinical-trial-industry-where-study-participants-say -theyre-incentivized-to-lie-even-about-medications-side-effects.

7: THE ORIGINS OF RESEARCH PARTICIPANT PROTECTION

1 "Nazi Medical Experiments," *Holocaust Encyclopedia* (United States Memorial Holocaust Museum, August 30, 2006), encyclopedia .ushmm.org/content/en/article/nazi-medical-experiments.

2 "The Nuremberg Trials," National WWII Museum, accessed December 2023, nationalww2museum.org/war/topics /nuremberg-trials.

3 Evelyne Shuster, "Fifty Years Later: The Significance of the Nuremberg Code," *New England Journal of Medicine* 337, no. 20 (1997): 1436–40.

4 "About the Untreated Syphilis Study at Tuskegee," CDC: U.S. Centers for Disease Control and Prevention, September 4, 2024, accessed February 19, 2025, cdc.gov/tuskegee/about/index.html.

5 National Commission for the Protection of Human Subjects of Biomedical and Behavioral Research, *The Belmont Report: Ethical Principles and Guidelines for the Protection of Human Subjects of Research* (Department of Health, Education, and Welfare, 1979), hhs.gov/ohrp/regulations-and-policy/belmont-report /read-the-belmont-report/index.html.

6 Allison Daniel, "Nutrition Researchers Saw Malnourished Children at Indian Residential Schools as Perfect Test Subjects," *The Conversation*, June 28, 2021, theconversation.com/nutrition -researchers-saw-malnourished-children-at-indian-residential-schools -as-perfect-test-subjects-162986; Brian Owens, "Canada Used Hungry Indigenous Children to Study Malnutrition," *Nature* (2013), nature.com/articles/nature.2013.13425; Ian Mosby, "Administering Colonial Science: Nutrition Research and Human Biomedical

Experimentation in Aboriginal Communities and Residential Schools, 1942–1952," *Histoire Sociale/Social History* 46, no. 91 (2013): 145–72; Zoe Tennant, "The Dark History of Canada's Food Guide: How Experiments on Indigenous Children Shaped Nutrition Policy," *Unreserved*, CBC Radio, April 19, 2021, cbc.ca/radio/unreserved /how-food-in-canada-is-tied-to-land-language-community-and-colonization-1.5989764/the-dark-history-of-canada-s-food-guide -how-experiments-on-indigenous-children-shaped-nutrition -policy-1.5989785.

7   Truth and Reconciliation Commission of Canada, *The Final Report of the Truth and Reconciliation Commission of Canada*, 6 vols. (McGill-Queen's University Press, 2015), nctr.ca/records/reports/#trc-reports.

8   Medical Research Council of Canada, *Celebrating the Medical Research Council of Canada: A Voyage in Time* (Public Works and Government Services Canada, 2000), publications.gc.ca/collections /Collection/MR21-19-2000E.pdf.

8: "CHANGE YOUR BRAIN WAVES; CHANGE YOUR LIFE!"

1   Michael Oleksyn, "Decolonization Is Part of the Culture at Riverside School," *SaskToday.ca*, May 27, 2023, sasktoday.ca/highlights /decolonization-is-part-of-the-culture-at-riverside-school-7060498.

2   Hengameh Marzbani et al., "Neurofeedback: A Comprehensive Review on System Design, Methodology and Clinical Applications," *Basic and Clinical Neuroscience Journal* 7, no. 2 (2016): 143–58.

3   Geoff Leo, "'No Consequences' for Violating Human Rights in Privately Funded Research in Canada, Says Ethics Expert," *CBC News*, December 2, 2024, cbc.ca/news/canada/saskatchewan /ethics-research-canada-privately-funded-1.7393063.

4   Geoff Leo, "Indigenous or Pretender?," *CBC News*, October 27, 2021, cbc.ca/newsinteractives/features/carrie-bourassa-indigenous.

5   Geoff Leo, "Inside the Brain School," *CBC News*, June 10, 2024, cbc.ca/newsinteractives/features/brain-school-study-indigenous -biocybernaut-james-hardt; "How a 'Bonkers' Brain Experiment Was Approved to Test on Indigenous Kids," *The National*, CBC, June 10, 2024, youtube.com/watch?v=pr6BVPMuT14&t=7s.

6 Leo, "Inside the Brain School."

7 Leo, "Inside the Brain School."

9: GOOD AND ETHICAL GOVERNANCE, PART I

1 Michael McDonald, *The Governance of Health Research Involving Human Subjects (HRIHS)* (Law Commission of Canada, 2000), publications.gc.ca/collections/collection_2008/lcc-cdc/JL2-45-2000E .pdf.

2 Leo, "Inside the Brain School."

3 Leo, "'No Consequences' for Violating."

4 "Scope," *TCPS Interpretations*, Government of Canada, last modified March 1, 2024, pre.ethics.gc.ca/eng/policy-politique _interpretations_scope-portee.html.

5 Leo, "'No Consequences' for Violating."

6 Leo, "'No Consequences' for Violating."

7 Fran Lowry, "Dr. Roger Poisson: 'I Have Learned My Lesson the Hard Way,'" *Canadian Medical Association Journal* 151, no. 6 (1994): 835–37, pmc.ncbi.nlm.nih.gov/articles/PMC1337145; Mackenzie Carpenter and Steve Twedt, "Anatomy of a Scandal," *Cancer Letter* 45, no. 41 (2019): 7–51, cancerletter.com/the-cancer-letter/20191101 _2.

8 U.S. Department of Justice, "U.S. Sues Canadian Hospital for $500,000 for Breast Cancer Research Fraud," news release, May 30, 1995, justice.gov/archive/opa/pr/Pre_96/May95/298.txt.html.

9 Pierre Deschamps et al., *Report on Control Mechanisms for Clinical Research in Québec*, October 1998 (original French version published July 1995), hracanada.org/wp-content/uploads/2022/04/Deschamps -Report-EN.pdf.

10 Michael McDonald, "Canadian Governance of Health Research Involving Human Subjects: Is Anybody Minding the Store?," *Health Law Journal* 9 (2001): 1–21, hracanada.org/wp-content /uploads/2025/03/M-McDonald-Is-Anybody-Minding-the-Store.pdf.

11 Miriam Shuchman, "Research Ethics Council Faces Dissolution," *Canadian Medical Association Journal* 182, no. 9 (2010): 890, doi.org /10.1503/cmaj.109-3254.

12 Senate Standing Committee on Social Affairs, Science and Technology, *Canada's Clinical Trial Infrastructure: A Prescription for Improved Access to New Medicines* (Senate of Canada, 2012), 25, 29, sencanada.ca/content/sen/committee/411/soci/rep/rep14nov12-e .pdf.

13 Anderson et al., "Research Ethics Broadly."

10: GOOD AND ETHICAL GOVERNANCE, PART II

1 "Clinical Trial Inspection Report Card Summary," Government of Canada, November 1, 2016, drug-inspections.canada.ca/gcp /fullReportCard-en.html?lang=en&gcpid=3cc094f0-6592-4a95 -bc44-b4b747cbab04#wb-auto-4.

2 "'Children at Ste-Justine Are Not Guinea Pigs': Hospital Defends Itself in Wake of Suspended Clinical Trial," *CBC News*, October 11, 2018, cbc.ca/news/canada/montreal/sainte-justine-study -suspended-by-health-canada-1.4852019; Pasquale Turbide, "Les cobayes de Sainte-Justine," *Enquête*, Radio-Canada, October 4, 2018, ici.radio-canada.ca/nouvelles/special/2018/10/hopital-sainte -justine-enfants-etudes-clinique-baclee-chercheurs-cancer-enquete -traitement-recherche-sante-canada; "Primum non nocere — D'abord ne pas nuire," *Enquête*, Radio-Canada, October 4, 2018, ici.radio-canada.ca/tele/enquete/site/segments/reportage/88505 /hopital-sainte-justine-recherche-enfants-cancer-protocole -pasquale-turbide.

3 "'Children at Ste-Justine.'"

4 "Detailed Information," Research Funding Decisions Database, Canadian Institutes of Health Research, webapps.cihr-irsc .gc.ca/decisions/p/main.html?lang=en#fq={!tag=allText}acallText %3ABittencourt&sort=namesort%20asc&start=0&rows=20.

5 Harry C. Rowsell, "Regulation of Animal Experimentation: Canada's Program of Voluntary Control," *Acta Physiologica Scandinavica* 128, no. S554 (1986): S95–S105.

6 "About the CCAC," Canadian Council on Animal Care, accessed February 20, 2025, ccac.ca/en/about/about-the-ccac.

7 Rowsell, "Regulation of Animal Experimentation."

8   Australian Commission on Safety and Quality in Health Care, *Literature Review: Quality Standards and Accreditation Schemes for Human Research Ethics Committees* (Australian Government Department of Health and Aged Care, 2023), safetyandquality.gov.au /sites/default/files/2023-06/pdf_for_publication_-_literature_review _dards_and_accreditation_schemes_for_human_research_ethics _committees_-_may_2023.pdf.

II: UNSAVOURY HEADWINDS

1   Richard Beckhard and Reuben T. Harris, *Organizational Transitions: Managing Complex Change* (Addison-Wesley, 1987).
2   "The Secretariat on Responsible Conduct of Research (SRCR): Terms of Reference," Panel on Responsible Conduct of Research, Government of Canada, last updated August 9, 2024, rcr.ethics.gc.ca /eng/srcr-scrr_staff-personnel.html.
3   Abraham H. Maslow, *The Psychology of Science: A Reconnaissance* (Harper & Row, 1966), 15–16.
4   "Agreement on the Administration of Agency Grants and Awards by Research Institutions," Government of Canada, September 17, 2020, science.gc.ca/site/science/en/interagency-research-funding /policies-and-guidelines/institutional-agreement.

CONCLUSION

1   Evans, "SFBC Drug Testers Have Tuberculosis."
2   Cribb et al., "Inside Canada's 'Exploitative' Clinical Trial Industry"; see also Maddi Dellplain, "Are Canada's Clinical Trials in Need of Reform? Experts Weigh In," *Healthy Debate*, October 23, 2024, healthydebate.ca/2024/10/topic/canadas-clinical-trials.
3   Leo, "'No Consequences' for Violating."
4   Catherine A. Schuppli and Michael McDonald, "Contrasting Modes of Governance for the Protection of Humans and Animals in Canada: Lessons for Reform," *Health Law Review* 13, no. 2–3 (2005): 97–106.

INDEX

ABOUT THE AUTHOR

Janice E. Parente has been a passionate advocate for the rights, safety, and welfare of research participants for over thirty years, fighting to strengthen protections and push for human research accreditation.

Born in Hamilton, Ontario, Janice earned a B.Sc. in biochemistry from McMaster University, followed by a Ph.D. in medicine (molecular pharmacology) at the University of Alberta and a post-doctoral fellowship at the University of Calgary. She began her career in clinical research within the pharmaceutical industry and, in 1992, founded a research company that grew into two successful operating companies. She later established two non-profits dedicated to Canadian human research accreditation and standards development.

Janice is the proud mother of two daughters, Adelaide and Halie Mei Jensen, both women in STEM pursuing postgraduate degrees. Janice lives with Olivia, her South Korean rescue dog, on a peaceful lake in the Quebec Laurentians.